THE STORY OF
CHANNON ROSE

LESSONS BETWEEN THE LINES

D1016067

CHANNON ROSE

ISBN-13: 978-1505462685

Book Cover Design & Layout by PIXEL eMarketing INC.

Legal Disclaimer

This book is dedicated to my mom.

Mom, I put you through hell and back (and that is an understatement), but you never gave up on me. You may have not always had time to deal with all my sh@t...being a single mom and raising two kids on your own while working full time, but somehow you always found a way to try to do what was best for me when I was making it virtually impossible for you. You are the strongest person I know, and I can only dream of one day being half as good a mom as you were to me. No words could ever express how thankful I am for all that you have done for me. I want you to know how blessed and honored I am to be able to call you my mother. Thank you, Mom, for all that you've done and all that you still do for me. I love you past forever.

My Beautiful Mother

Contents

Welcome to the Asylum

My name is Channon Rose. You might know me from my YouTube videos where I post daily blogs, product reviews, makeup tutorials and fashion tips. Or you may recognize me from hosting Playboy TV or the viral sex tape I was in with Paris Hilton called "One Night in Paris." I now lead a comfortable, laid back life with my fiancé and Bengal cat. But it was not always that way. Any story worth telling is grounded in truth, even if that truth is uglier than you would like to admit, and I admit mine was pretty ugly. While many of the things that I experienced as a child were traumatic and disturbing, I would like you to remember my story is one of growth and discovery, making mistakes and then recovering from them, and eventually finding myself amongst the chaos. Let's just say I had a pretty f**cked up childhood. I know most people do, but I wanted to share my story with you so you can not only get to know me a little better but I also hoped it will maybe help someone out there that may have been through similar struggles.

This book is for everyone, whether it be for entertainment purposes, to get to know me better, or maybe reading this book will make you feel less alone. Most importantly, if you know someone that would benefit from reading my story, please pass this book along to them. I wrote this not only for my own therapy but to help others learn from my mistakes. This is an account of my childhood years and the many lessons I learned along the way. I hope you find some wisdom among my chaos. This is my story— well, at least the first 6,570 days of it.

Welcome to the asylum.

ME

Chapter 1

Kicking & Screaming in Silence

"The greatest trick the devil ever pulled
was convincing the world he didn't exist."

SUFFOCATION

When I think back to my childhood I remember mostly negative aspects of my life in which my stepmother secretly verbally and physically abused me. I was eight years old when my parents got divorced. My dad cheated on my mother with a so-called "Christian" woman who was my moms best friend and who was also married at the time with two children of her own. Her name was Misty, and for most of my childhood I blamed her for everything that went wrong in my life.

For me, there is no such thing as silence. In my quietest moments, my mind fills with images, emotions, and pain from the past. I was born on September 16, 1985, in Northridge, California. I had a 50% chance of even being born. My parents weren't together for very long before my mother found out she was pregnant.

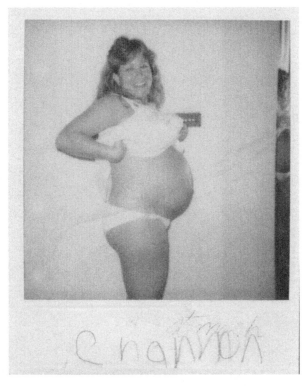

My mom pregnant with me

At the time they were just dating so my mom told my dad that she wasn't going to have the baby unless they got married. My parents ended up getting married when my mom was three months pregnant.

My mom and dad on their wedding day

Yes, I am an abortion survivor. I believe many people are these days, although they are rarely told about it. So thanks dad for letting me be born! When it came around time to bring me into the world I was a breech baby, which means I was in the feet first position in my moms tummy. Normally, babies come out headfirst so the doctors scheduled a C-section. Coming out feet first, kicking and screaming, was not part of the plan. I was born at 4:11 AM and there was a reason I was breech and not ready to come out naturally, it is because I am not a morning person, and definitely not a 4:11 in the morning, morning person. Hello, I wasn't ready to come out that early, I wanted to sleep in!

The C-section went smoothly and my mom cried happy tears when she held me for the first time.

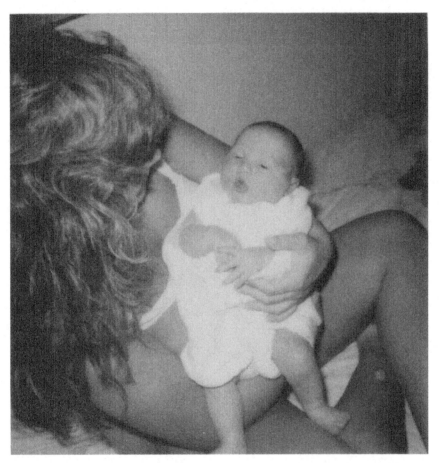

Picture of my mom holding me as a baby

I was her first-born child. My mother was a beautiful blonde-haired, blue-eyed surgical technician. She had moved from Miami, Florida where she had lived her whole life, to Los Angeles, California to work for a world-renowned plastic surgeon in Beverly Hills. She didn't have any other family in Los Angeles other than her sister (my Aunt Jen), who had also moved to LA to work and start her own company.

Both my aunt and dad were there when I was born, and my Aunt Jen became one of the main people who took care of me when I was a baby because my mom had to work a lot. Recalling my actual childhood has always been a struggle—not because it is hard to remember but because it is so vivid, like a running movie of my life.

My mother and father had met through a mutual friend at a local restaurant called Friday's. My father was 10 years older than my mother and my mom didn't really like him when they first met. She wasn't attracted to him and he was too "crazy" for her. I think he just wasn't mature enough for her taste and was living life more on the wild side. He was a total adrenaline junkie. That same evening that they met, my dad asked my mother and her friend if they would like to go out on my dad's boat the next morning. My mother said, "no way!" to her friend, but despite that, when the call from my father came at 7 a.m. the next morning, she was at that lake.

My dad must have been driving his boat really fast to impress my mom, but instead it just scared her, so she told him to drop her off on shore. I asked her how they ended up together if the first and second impression were so bad. My mom said he grew on her, and eventually they fell in love.

Three years after my parents had me, my little sister Birdy was born on Christmas day. It was also the very first day that it snowed in Los Angeles— December 25th, 1988. I was so excited to meet

My mom and dad happy and in love

her. I have clear memories of the day I met my sister. I was only three years old and I wore an oversized t-shirt to the hospital that read "Big Sister". My mom even let me hold my baby sister! Birdy was given to my mom in a great big Christmas stocking—how cool is that!? I remember sharing Lipton soup with my mom in the hospital, thinking how yummy it was, and I remember it being such a happy day for our family.

My father already had two kids from two previous marriages and now two with my mom for a total of four kids. Life was great and having a big family was fun. My mom was still working for the plastic surgeon, and my dad owned his own business as an electrical contractor. They both made decent money, and we lived very comfortably. We were never super rich, but we were never poor.

Chanel and I

We were fortunate enough to always have a roof over our heads and food on the table. Being wealthy or poor doesn't always equate to a great or terrible childhood. Things can happen, whether you have money or not. At this point in my life though, life was simple and uncomplicated. We were happy, and family life was great.

I was never close with my older half-brother Patrick; he was much older than me and had his own life. But I was close with Chanel, my older half-sister, even though she lived in Texas with her mom (my aunt Boni).

I loved her so much, and all the times that she was in Los Angeles to visit she practically raised me.

Chanel and I still joke to this day about how it is crazy that my little sister and I are still alive because she would be left alone to take care of us when she was still a child herself. We laugh about how carefree my mom was, and talk about me having green poop for weeks after I ate all the leaves off a houseplant. Apparently I was left alone in my crib, which was within reach of the plant. I guess that plant must have tasted pretty good! Chanel ended up being like a second mom, friend, and sister all rolled into one. She was the one who taught me about my period, how to use tampons and pads, and even how to wash my hair. She would play with me all the time and I loved that. I will always have a lot of respect and love for her and be forever grateful because of that. I felt so lucky to be able to call her my sister and I still do today.

Ever since I can remember I always wanted my mom to take pictures and videos of me, it didn't matter what I was doing I just wanted to be in the spot light. I loved performing, putting on shows for my family, and singing. It made my soul happy. My mom filmed and took tons of pictures and videos of me as a child. I loved modeling and acting even from a young age. I have the pictures to prove it.

*Me wearing purple lipstick
and posing in lingerie*

Me playing dress up and modeling in our backyard, how awesome is that outfit?

Me dressed as a playboy bunny for Halloween

Both of my parents were laid back and liberal, my mother especially. She was amazing and never overbearing. My father was the same way, though he didn't have a problem with discipline and spanking, so my baby sister and I were very well behaved. Both our parents worked long hours so we had nannies, au pairs, and babysitters that helped raise us when our parents were away. One of my favorite nannies was Maria. Maria was Hispanic, and the most caring nanny I had. She made the best Mexican food, taught me to speak Spanglish, and took very good care of me. I remember she would put this Mexican salt stuff called Lucas or Tajin on my popcorn and fruit and I loved it! I still put (I call it Mexican Candy Salt) it on everything.

My early days were fun and surrounded by family and friends. My parents believed in a good education, so both my sister and I were placed in private Christian schools. The first school I ever attended was Pinecrest. Like most kids, I did not want to be left at school on the first day of Kindergarten. I was the kid who screamed and cried and held onto my mom's leg as she was trying to leave me at school. Eventually I allowed her to leave and by the end of the day when she came to pick me up I didn't want to go home. I remember they had green eggs and ham at school that day, I thought the green eggs were so cool and I loved the book they read to us which was the famous Dr. Seuss book Green Eggs and Ham. Then we did arts and crafts and I loved doing crafts. I remember drawing or writing and the teachers always taking my crayon or pencil out of my left hand and putting it into my right hand. I always switched it back though, as I was clearly left-handed. Thinking back on it, I got upset that the teachers did that but I think it was mostly because everything is made for right-handed people and they were just trying to make my life easier. Little did they know I would grow up and learn EVERYTHING the hard way. I have to say I love being left-handed though. I am convinced by the studies done that lefties are more creative and organized. I think it's very true and I love being creative. Art and creativity was very natural for me, but when it came to memorizing my ABC's I had a more difficult time than the other kids. I was a slow learner, but far from stupid. To be honest, school was always pretty difficult for me. I did not learn as quickly as the other children, and I felt like there was something wrong with me. My teachers suggested I go to a place called Learning Lab because I had a hard time keeping up in my classes. The one thing I struggled with the most was numbers. They just instantly make my brain go nuts because I don't understand math, no matter how hard someone tries to explain it to me. My brain is just allergic to math. I didn't get it then, and I don't get it now. Thankfully, we have calculators, computers, accountants, and bank tellers or I would be a lost cause.

I attended Kindergarten, first, and second grade at Pinecrest. I had a best friend in the beginning of grade school, her name was Allison and we did everything together. Some of my favorite childhood memories are of Allison and I going to summer camp at Pinecrest. I loved going to summer camp, we would do talent shows, plays, and go on overnight camping trips! We did a lot of crafts and swam in the pool, it was so much fun!

By second grade, I was getting bullied a lot for having clubbed thumbs, and I wasn't doing as well in my classes. It got so bad that I asked my mom if I could switch schools because I was very unhappy there. My mom agreed and put me into

School Picture

Valley Presbyterian School in the third grade. I was still struggling a lot in school at VPS but the kids were much nicer and I made friends fast. I really liked that school, although most of the work was difficult for me. The worst part was that my parents were unable to help me with my schoolwork because they either didn't have time or they didn't know how to do it themselves.

I didn't learn how to tell time correctly until the sixth grade! That is an experience I will never forget. A friend of mine, Becky, once asked me what time it was, and I froze up. I did not know. She was the most popular girl in school and one of my best friends. Without making me feel like a huge idiot, she taught me how to tell time during recess. That was really nice of her, and something I'll never forget.

Valley Presbyterian School was a very religious school and both my sister and I attended there.

My little sister had a friend named Vicky, whose mom would drop us off after school because my parents worked late. It turned out that Vicky's mother Misty was having an affair with my father, which is why she always did "favors" for my mom. She also happened to be my mom's best friend at the time. Eventually my mom found out about the affair and asked my dad for a divorce. My father did not know it yet, but he was making the biggest mistake of his life, and mine.

My sister and I

At this point my parent's were technically separated but we all still lived together while my mom was looking for a place for us to live. I was devastated when I found out my parents would be getting a divorce. No one else's parents at my school had gotten a divorce and I felt like an outcast and like I didn't fit in. Everyone else seemed to have perfect lives at home or so I thought. One day after school I remember walking into my parents' bedroom and they were having sex. At least I assumed that was what they were doing. I quickly ran out so they wouldn't know I saw them. I felt confused but happy because I thought my parents would be getting back together and we wouldn't have to move anymore. Later that day, my dad took my sister and I out for "ice cream" but instead we ended up at Misty's house. When we got there I was so upset and didn't understand why my dad would lie and do that to my mom. I went into the laundry room where Misty was doing laundry and told Misty that my mom and dad had sex before we got there. I wanted her to know that my parents loved each other. What she was doing with my dad was wrong. She just looked at me with a disgusted look on her face.

I would live to regret telling her that. That decision backfired on me big time, as Misty flew into a rage and confronted my dad right away. "Tell her you are lying!" my father insisted as he tried to convince Misty it was a lie. "But I saw you bouncing up and down on mommy!" I replied in my eight-year-old voice. He continued to talk his way out of a lie, but Misty wouldn't buy it. So my father turned his frustration towards me. He bent me over and spanked me really hard, multiple times urging me to confess it wasn't true. But I didn't want to lie, I was telling the truth so he continued to spank me harder and harder until I couldn't take it anymore. Finally I screamed, "It's a lie!" I had to make the pain stop. My dad calls this "beating it out of you".

After my spankings, I was sent to sit in the corner facing the wall, away from everyone else. The spankings were not enough to get my father's point across. The back of my butt and legs were beat red and were stinging badly. I could barely sit because my little butt was burning and throbbing and I was in so much pain. I remember sitting in that corner sobbing and thinking that my dad hated me and loved Misty more than me. I missed my mom and hoped that she would come to get me but she thought we were out getting ice cream. A few minutes had passed when my dad, my sister, Misty and her kids went to watch TV in another room.

As soon as they left I got up as fast as I could to find a phone to call my mom. When she answered, I told her where I was. I was crying so much I could barely catch my breath to talk. I told her, "Dad spanked me really hard can you come get me?" Misty must have heard me on the phone and told my dad, who stormed into the room demanding answers. I told him I wanted my Mom to come to pick me up. I didn't realize it then, but my dad was a womanizer, or player you might say. He had played Misty and my mother, making them believe they were the "only" ones.

My actions made my father furious. I was a troublemaker in his eyes. He grabbed the phone and threw it then started spanking me even worse. I was getting spanked over and over in the same spot he had hit me before. The pain was overwhelming. I was screaming in pain and had tears running down my face. My mother heard my screams on the other end of the phone and dropped everything to come get me. I can't imagine how my mother must have felt getting a call from her ex-best friends house after my dad had told her he was taking us kids for ice cream and had just finished having sex with her hours before. She must have been shocked to hear me on the other end crying and begging her to come get me. Misty lived a short distance away, so my mom arrived quickly. My mom burst into the house and began shouting at my father and Misty. The three of them ended up in the bathroom and slammed the door shut, but the four of us kids (Misty's two children, my sister and I) could all still hear them fighting. The screaming and shouting grew louder, and then I could hear someone getting thrown against a wall. I was scared, all of us kids were. I was the oldest, so I called 911 for help. My mom had taught me about emergencies, and I was in fear for my mother's safety. After what felt like an hour, my mom came out of the bathroom crying and extremely upset. Her hair, make-up, and clothes were a total mess. She immediately grabbed my sister and I, we rushed to her car and all three of us cried on the drive home.

I wasn't there to witness what happened next, but apparently after we left, several cop cars and a helicopter surrounded Misty's house. That night was only the beginning of what Misty would use against me later on. Once things died down, my heartbroken mom had to find a place to live and figure out how to raise two kids all on her own. The man she loved had been cheating on her, with her best friend. She had to stay at my dad's house out of need, which was painful. They fought constantly, and it was a very messy divorce. My sister and I had to see all of it. Thankfully, my little sister wasn't quite old enough to really understand what was going on. But I did.

Day in and day out my sister and I heard them fight. One night in particular was really bad, and I heard my mom shout, "Let me go!"

I ran into the kitchen to see if she was okay. My dad was dragging her on the floor by her hair. "Stop hurting my mom!" I screamed. "We were just playing" my dad replied. I knew that was a lie. I was furious with my father. My mom got off the floor, hugged me, and told me she was fine. A few days later my mom moved us out of my dads and into a townhouse. Once we had moved out, it hit me. My parents didn't love each other anymore and they were never going to be together again. I remember sitting in my room staring out the window crying because I knew things would never be the same. I was torn apart on the inside, just like my family was on the outside. I was eight years old and I didn't understand why all of this was happening and why my parent's didn't love each other anymore. Custody was given to my mom, and we were with my dad each Thursday, Friday, and every other weekend. My dad had to pay child support, which was something he had an issue with years prior from a previous divorce. Apparently he wasn't making child support payments for my older half-sister Chanel and because of that, the police had come and taken him away in handcuffs. I was pretty young when that happened but I witnessed the whole thing and screamed at the police in my dad's defense to leave him alone and to let him go. He made good money, so I never understood why he didn't pay. I know now that he was very irresponsible with money. My mom ended up paying Chanel's child support and sorting out all the family finances. Now I know so far my dad sounds like a monster, but I want to say he did do many good things for us kids. Now that I'm older I'm closer to my dad than I've ever been and have a great relationship with him, but growing up was much different and things got really bad before they got better. He did always keep a roof over our head, provided food for us, bought us clothes, paid for us to go to good schools, and he also taught me how to play sports.

This is the lesson I learned:

No one's life is perfect. Some lives are worse than others, but what I learned in this situation is that you cannot choose your parents. Instead of dwelling on all the bad things about them, in the future, try to think of what they *did do* for you. My dad was not perfect by any stretch of the imagination, but he did make sure that I had a home, toys, and food. He made sure I was going to a good school, and he taught me a lot of the sports that I still love to this day. Take the good from the bad, and your life will not seem so awful after all. There is *always* something good to take from a negative situation, and you should try to train your brain to think good things, no matter how hard it seems at the time. If I can do it, then so can you.

Chapter 2

My Shattered Fairytale

"Children are like wet cement; whatever
falls on them makes an impression."
DR. HAIM GINOTT

Misty was now my dad's new girlfriend. I never understood what he saw in her. My mom was so much better looking than her, so for my dad to be leaving my mom for this other woman just didn't make any sense. I know it's not nice to talk bad about someone's appearance but she wasn't a nice person so I'm just going to say it like it is. Misty was very off-putting and unattractive. Of course I had a bias against her, and I despised her the minute I knew she was a main cause in my parent's separation, but even if that wasn't the case, I could say the same thing about her appearance. She had brown frizzy hair, brown eyes, and was slightly overweight. There really wasn't a wow factor in her looks. She wasn't tall, she wasn't thin, and she didn't have amazing eyes. This was not the fairytale life I was hoping for. My young mind could not make sense of my dad's betrayal. My mother was an excellent wife and a better mom—she worked very hard and took care of our family. Misty had two kids of her own, Vicky and Terry. My little sister Birdy was the same age as Vicky, and Terry was a few years younger. We all knew each other because we were family friends, went to the same private Christian school, and played many of the same sports together.

At Valley Presbyterian School, Christianity and religion was a large influence in our daily lives. Every single day before school started the entire school would stand outside lined up by grade in the quad area in front of our school and we would pledge our allegiance to the American flag, and also pledge our allegiance to the Christian flag. On Mondays we had to attend chapel, Sundays we would go to church, and before each new subject in school we would pray as well. It was a very religious school. It was a little weird to me, because my family was the least religious family out of everyone I knew at the time. In fact, our family wasn't religious at all. I think my parents just sent us there because they wanted a better education for us, wanted us to stay out of trouble, and it was the closest private school to our house. I have to say though I really liked that school. The teachers were nice, I had a lot of good friends, and I got to sing in choir class, which was something I loved. We did a lot of school plays, which were fun as well. Our classes were much smaller than in public schools, which was helpful as I do better in a more one on one learning environment. Still, I always felt a bit different than the other kids and it always bothered me a lot.

They say lefties think with the right side of their brain, so that could explain why I felt so different from everyone else. I don't know if I was actually different than the other kids, or just thought differently than the other kids. I don't have ADD or ADHD—at least I was never officially diagnosed with it at the time—but I struggled to understand what the teacher was trying to teach me. When the teacher focused on me in a one-on-one environment and took the time to explain it to me, I would understand it. I learned things differently from the other kids, and I think each of us learn in different ways. Special attention was something I needed to learn something properly. The teachers at that school were very caring and understanding—they knew what I needed and were very helpful. That's the biggest reason I enjoyed going to Valley Presbyterian and it was probably my favorite school I attended.

The hardest part about going to school was waking up for school. I hated the early mornings, and still hate early mornings to this day. I have always been a total night owl. My brain wakes up at night, and it's also when I'm most creative and productive. In an effort to minimize getting up early as a kid, I developed a system that allowed me to sleep a little more—by dressing in my school clothes the night before. Sleeping in my school uniform, even with my socks and shoes on, to get an extra 20 minutes or so of sleep. I had a pretty good little system going until one day my mom caught me doing it. My mother had noticed one evening that I was trying to fall asleep fully dressed in my school clothes. She made me change into my pajamas and made me promise to never do it again.

I got away with it for awhile since my mom and dad were usually gone by the time my sister and I were ready for school. My father owned his own electrical company so every morning there was a bunch of Hispanic workers that would wait outside our house and drive these work trucks provided by my dad to go to their jobs. My dad was always busy so my dad's workers would drop us off at school. I was always so embarrassed to get dropped off at school in an old work truck. You know the work trucks I'm referring to; they were white, dented, beat up, toolboxes on the sides and long ladders sticking out the back. The other kids were dropped off in fancy cars by their parents, while I would exit a work truck smelling like exhaust fumes. As you might guess, after awhile I told my dad's workers to drop us off a block away from school so nobody would see us getting out of the beat up work trucks. I was always so embarrassed by that.

When I would see the other kids at school getting out of their parents' nice cars, I always thought they had great parents and that they were setting good examples for their children. I thought since I was going to a religious Christian school, the parent's were probably good people too right? Christians were supposed to lead by example and love one another, and be faithful in their marriage to their husband or wife, but that was far from the truth. Up until then I believed in God. I thought how could God be real and let this happen? I started to think it was all just one big lie. I lost faith that day and I've struggled with it immensely since that day forward. It didn't help that Misty was that "nice Christian" woman my dad introduced me to. I'll never forget the day Misty and her two kids moved into my dad's house.

She had been my Christian role model, and now here she was cheating on her faithful husband with whom she had two kids and leaving him for my married father. She ripped her two kids away from their dad to put them with mine. Since my sister and I spent most of our time at our mom's house it felt like my dad had a new family that took our place. It hurts to feel like that and when we were there, Misty demanded all my dad's attention. Misty did not love my dad; she was clinically obsessed with him. My sister, my mom, and I were replaced. I was the oldest child, and that came with a lot of awareness, guilt, and pressure. I wasn't aware of everything, but I was old enough to understand much of what was occurring, as the other kids and my sister were much younger and it's hard to comprehend the reality of situations at such a young age. As time passed, I would spend more of it with Misty—who was fast becoming the most horrible person I had ever encountered. She was just a terrible human being. But I was raised to respect my elders, so I began to swallow her abusive nature.

Misty would not tolerate my father giving me any attention; instead she chose to manipulate situations to cut me out so that she could have him all to herself. Her jealousy was powerful, and it was totally crazy. My dad barely gave me any attention anyway, but she made sure the few times that he did offer some, she would sweep it away. My dad wasn't affectionate with us kids, he worked all the time and was emotionally distant. From the age of eight years old, I have no memories of him ever telling me he loved me, hugging me, or even asking about my day at school. Perhaps he resented me for causing problems early on with him and Misty, or perhaps six kids did not leave much time for affection. The only time he did spend with me was on the sports field, where he coached our teams. He was a good coach but hard on us. I played basketball, soccer, volleyball, and softball and I was always the best player on the team since I practiced so much.

The coach's kids are usually the best players on the team so I felt that pressure to do better than everyone else. I strived for perfection. I wanted to be the best to make my dad proud, but most of all I just wanted his attention. Any attention after the divorce would have been nice, but it rarely came my way. Being the best in sports was just expected. Sports meant everything to my dad. With both parents working hard, long hours, we were placed in after school care and early morning care. I only got to spend an hour or two with my parents at night, and on the weekends I would play sports and see friends. Attention was something that wasn't given out freely, or there simply wasn't time for attention. Gaining love and attention from my parent's for doing something great is what I wanted, but it didn't happen that way.

Then, I learned something new. Doing bad things got my parents' attention. It got to a point later on where I did not care what kind of attention I got, as long as I got some attention I was happy. Misty understood this, but with four kids in the house, attention was not something she was willing to give up. It was always about her and her happiness, and she was willing to do anything to get my dad's attention. Misty slowly but surely started verbally abusing me the first year she moved in with my dad. It began with little things—she kept mentioning that I was too chubby and needed to lose weight.

My sister and I fishing, this is when
Misty was telling me I was overweight

Looking back at photos, I was skinny, and she was the one who needed to lose some weight. She would tell me that my nose was big, and it actually was a little big so when she would say hurtful things like that it made it much worse. It made me self-conscious because my dad would make fun of my nose too. However, Misty was very careful to never say anything bad to me when other people were around. She wasn't stupid when it came to manipulation, and when you're a young girl like I was; it's even easier for an adult to win at that game. One time on the way home from school, she picked up McDonald's for everyone—Happy Meals for the kids. I was so excited to get my toy! A bunch of my friends at school had the toys from McDonalds and I wanted one so bad. I was so excited when I found out we were getting Happy Meals because now I would get a toy too! My dad had to work late that night, which Misty knew. When we all got home and sat down to eat, there was no Happy Meal for me. Keep in mind my dad wasn't home to see this. I was so distraught that I wasn't getting a Happy Meal and I was even more upset that everyone got a toy but me. When I asked her where my Happy Meal was, she told me that she didn't order me one because I was too fat for a Happy Meal. She made me eat a bologna sandwich instead while I watched all the other kids enjoy their McDonald's Happy Meals and play with their new toys that night. This may not seem like a big deal to most people but I was so young and it was very upsetting to me. Misty did things like this to me all the time. Misty knew I absolutely hated bologna. I personally believe this is where my eating disorders stemmed from. Constantly being told I'm too fat even though I wasn't, and being denied to eat meals with the rest of the family.

Even though I was skinny, Misty did her best to condition me to believe that I was fat. Every day she would find new ways to tell me how fat I was getting. Over and over, again and again—all I could do was listen. At that age, you soak up everything like a sponge. Misty had stepped into my life and had convinced me that I was grossly overweight. Eventually, I started to believe her and I was convinced I was fat. The abuse continued, and moved into every aspect of my life. Sometimes we would go to the store, and Misty would buy toys for everyone but me because I was a "bad girl" even though I had not done anything wrong. She had also decided that she would never allow me to sit next to her in the front seat of the car. I was made to sit in the back while the younger kids got to take turns on the way back home from school. This escalated, as abuse does. Whenever one of the kids got in trouble, she would blame it on me even though it was never my fault. The stories were fake and made up to make my father believe that I was a bad child when, really, I was a great kid. Misty was raising me in hatred, abusing me because I reminded her of my mother and because of the night I told her that my mom and dad were having sex. Each time she blamed, excluded, or taunted me; I accepted it—not knowing any better as a young child. I started to feel like a loser, unloved, self-conscious, and that I wasn't a good little girl. With each hurtful and demeaning gesture made towards me, I would also be told that it was for my own good and that my parents think the same bad things about me but they don't want to tell me anything negative because they don't want to hurt my feelings. So, Misty would say that she was only trying to help me, and she was the only one telling me the truth.

Then I was put in the middle of my mom and Misty's immature games with each other. When I was at my mom's house she would call Misty a cow because she was overweight. This was a horrible thing to do, especially in front of me. My mom was so hurt by what was happening, and the fact that it was her best friend who ruined her marriage and betrayed her made it even worse. My mother would call my dad's house and when Misty would pick up the phone she would tell me to say "Moo" and then we would hang up. Then Misty would say awful things to me about my mother when I was at my dad's house. This went on for awhile between them. Misty would send my mom singles ads in the newspaper that she highlighted in bright colors, implying that she needed to date and get over my dad. It was awful and I was right in the middle of it all. It sucked.

I still don't completely understand why Misty targeted me with everything; I was only a child. She became openly mean to me, hurting my feelings any chance she got. She came to our softball games and humiliated, belittled, and embarrassed me—asking me if I had showered because I stank— in front of my entire team. When she said things like that all the girls on my team would laugh at me and make jokes about me for the entire season. She wanted me to feel unloved and unwanted, and it worked. She was systematically, clinically, and progressively destroying my self-esteem.

My fairytale at this stage was shattered. I became self-conscious, crippled by the idea that I was fat, ugly, and an evil person. All I wanted was love, attention, and for my parents to be proud of me, but instead, my evil stepmother had her revenge. I lived through years of violent verbal and emotional abuse from that woman. I was young, I didn't know any better, and I didn't know how to find help.

Eventually, after years of abuse, I believed the bad things Misty always told me. Once that happened, I started acting out. When Misty would start to abuse me, I would give her a little attitude back. I was so sick of her constantly treating me poorly and I finally wanted to stick up for myself. I was suffocating. The other kids were the only ones that knew and saw the abuse that Misty did to me but they were very young and too scared to do anything, so they kept their mouths shut. That's when the verbal abuse started escalating to physical abuse.

It was a Sunday morning and we were getting ready for church, as Misty was a self-proclaimed "woman of God." She'd been ironing my dad's blue collared shirt when I walked past her to use the restroom. As I walked by her, she turned and burned me with the iron, pushing it hard onto the bare skin of my arm. I screamed and asked her what the heck she was doing. "An accident," she said to me calmly with a fake smile. I was in pain, physically and emotionally. My arm was throbbing, and started to turn red. I could smell my burnt skin. I couldn't believe what she had done to me. I tried to tell my dad but he didn't believe me, and thought I was just making things up and trying to get attention or be dramatic. He believed Misty when she said it was an accident. I should have gone to the hospital my burn was so severe, but that wasn't an option because Misty was a nurse. She could fix me up, and after all why spend money at the hospital when she could give me the same care at home she said to my father. I remember not being able to look at her as she was wrapping gauze around my burn. It was like she believed her own lies. She acted as if it was a total accident. Unbelievable, I thought to myself. I was scared of her. She was crazy!

After that, she did everything she could to lay her hands on me. She would beat me with belts, spank me until I could barely walk, slap me across the face, or give me a time out and force me to sit in the corner for hours. These larger incidents of course happened when my dad was away, and they occurred for no reason at all other than the fact of her being able to do it and get away with it. When my dad was around, she was the loving, caring stepmother. When he was not around, she was an evil witch. I never told my mother because I believed the abuse would come back tenfold. I was too scared to think of what would even come next if I told anyone. But this was only the beginning.

These are the lessons that I learned:

- If you or someone you know is being abused, *tell someone* and *get help;* do not feed into his or her scare tactics and let it continue, because it can get much worse. It is not okay to be verbally or physically abused by *anyone.* Tell a teacher, a family friend—anyone that you know and trust. Get help; you deserve it, and people do care about you, whether you know it or not.

- Just because someone is nice in front of people does not mean that they are not abusive behind closed doors. There are sick people in this world, and there are tons of people out there that love to watch others suffer, even kids.

- Abusers are proficient at making their target feel helpless and unable to tell anyone or if they do, things will become infinitely worse for them. These are not idle threats, but they are also not reasons to not say anything. Abuse escalates, and the longer you leave it, the more comfortable abusers get at carrying out their crimes.

- Abusers are often the nicest, most incredible people around company they want to impress. They can be charming and most are very smart and manipulative. When you scratch beneath the surface though, they have major control, attention, and psychiatric issues. At heart, they are deeply insecure and have an overblown ego that cannot be challenged. Know these signs, and protect yourself from these people.

- Some people raise their kids the way they were raised because it is all they know; break this cycle if you were abused as a child. Do not let your kids live the miserable life you did. Give them what you never had: love and attention.

Chapter 3

Drugged Up in the Asylum

"Jail was preferable. In jail they only
limit you physically. In the mental ward
they tampered with your soul and mind."

JOHN KENNEDY TOOLE

Misty was becoming confident in her abuse as the years went by and as I got older it inevitably got worse. I progressively started to give her more attitude, but now I did it in front of others like my sister, her kids, and my dad, whereas before it was just somewhat between her and I when nobody else was around. Since nobody really knew the truth, or they turned a blind eye, when I would outright give attitude to Misty they thought I was being mean to her because she broke my parents up. My father would get extremely upset with me when I was rude to Misty. He would tell me to treat her with more respect. I tried to tell him about how abusive she was, but he never believed me. My father believed that I was telling stories to split them up. Clearly Misty was manipulating my fathers mind as well. She groomed him for anything that I could have said to him so she would never get caught. I wish he would have believed me, just once. When I did try to tell my parents, my father would just end up getting mad, and when I told my mother she would call my dad which of course would get my dad mad at me again. It ended up causing a lot of drama, so I eventually stopped telling them anything regarding Misty. I was still very young and so I slowly came to think that stuff like this was typical within families. That was my life during those years and I believed it was normal so that became my thought process of why my parents never did anything about it. Until the night Misty tried to kill me.

I had no one to talk to, so I turned to writing. It was a way to get things out in the open, express myself, and release some of my feelings. It was my own kind of therapy I had found comfort in and it made me feel better. One night I was home alone with Misty; I dreaded these days when I was left alone at home with her. Everyone else was at a basketball game that my dad was coaching but I had to stay home to do homework. I already had a rough day, mostly because of some very hurtful things that Misty had said to me earlier in the day. She said that my dad loved her family more than mine and that's why I stay with my mom most of the time and if my dad had it his way he would never see us because he doesn't like my mom and we remind him of her. She explained that he simply doesn't have time for us. She also told me that my dad said I was mistake in the first place and that he wished he never had me or married my mom. What Misty told me hurt my heart beyond belief. How could anyone say this to a little girl? Her manipulative rants were so evil, and her being my elder, I believed them. I blamed Misty and not my dad, because I loved my dad, and thought none of this would have ever happened if she hadn't come into the picture. Who could I talk to? Was what she was saying true? I was alone, afraid, scared, confused, and felt deeply unloved. The calm I found was during my writing, so that same day I wrote a poem about all the hurt I was feeling. I eventually turned my poem into a song.

(You can download the full song that I wrote and sang on iTunes https://itunes.apple.com/us/ album/missy/ id910981211?i=910981267)

Mommy and Daddy they're fighting again,
I remember the day it all began.
It started with her; she looked like a witch,
Yes it started with her; she turned out a bitch,
She took my mom away from my dad,
and she made our family hurt so bad,
Misty, you amaze me, you are crazy,
Daddy, it's like a war over you,
But Daddy she's winning, she's obsessed with you,
Daddy, I wish you could see, Misty is destroying our family,
Daddy, she hurts me physically, I really wish you'd listen to me,
Misty, you amaze me, you are crazy.

This next part of the poem was added years later when I made this poem into a song.

Daddy thank you for listening to me,
She was so close to killing me,
I thank God everyday for you leaving her,
today she's in jail for manslaughter,
I won't forget how she ruined me,
But she taught me a lot of what not to be.

I had left my room to use the restroom, and when I came back, Misty was in my room reading my poem with tears streaming down her face. She wasn't sad; she was angry—shaking with anger. I was shocked and petrified. Misty stared at me with her piercing brown eyes as if the world stopped and every ounce of her focus, hatred, anger and disgust was focused directly at me. In that moment, nothing in the world could have pulled her focus away from me. Her eyes almost looked as if they went black as she stared at me as if she wanted to kill me.

In an eerily calm voice she said, "I want you to tear this up, throw it away, and I don't ever want to see it again." I was terrified but at the same time I was furious that she had invaded my privacy, gone into my room, and read my diary. I responded in a trembling voice, "No, that is my personal stuff, it's mine, and I want to keep it"! It was the first time I had blatantly refused to act on her orders, but I couldn't believe the words that fell out of my mouth. As soon as I responded back to her, I wanted to take my words back. I swallowed hard and was so nervous for what was going to happen next. I knew she was going to hurt me, I just didn't know how, or what was coming this time. We were home alone; I had no one there to help me. She could do whatever she wanted to me. Misty was smart, and she had figured out ways of hiding the physical and verbal abuse she had done to me. I knew something was coming my way, and here I was, a little girl about to be severely punished, beaten, or possibly much worse. One thing I did know is that Misty would find a way to put all the blame on me for whatever was about to happen.

I was too afraid to say what she had read to her face, which is why I wrote it in my diary to begin with. Everything went dead quiet, and then she stepped towards me. I took a step back. She stepped towards me again. I took another step back, but now I was stuck, my back was against the wall. Misty took another step towards me. I had run out of room. I was trapped. She was now within inches of me. I was now face to face with her when she screamed, "I'm not going to play your games little girl, you will throw this f★★king paper away NOW!" I had never seen this kind of intensity from her before. I could feel her anger, it was unlike anything I'd felt or seen from her before.

I yelled back at her "No, I don't want to!" I don't know what I was thinking, but I was still sticking up for myself because I knew either way I was going to get hurt. Misty threw the paper onto the ground, grabbed my arms, and violently threw me to the ground. Before I could do anything she got on top of me, and pinned me down to the hard ground. She started screaming "How could you write these things about me you little b★★ch! How could you say these horrible things you stupid little c★★t! Don't you see how happy I make your father?! These are all lies! Is that what you want, your parents back together? Is this your way of trying to get rid of me?! I will never let that happen you little piece of s★★t!" as she spit on me.

She would scream nasty things to me and spit in my face. I remember the taste of her salty tears as they dropped from her eyes onto my face and into my mouth. She was frantically screaming, crying, and trembling all at the same time. I wanted so badly to wipe away her nasty spit and tears off of me, but she had my arms pinned to the ground, she was squeezing my tiny arms so hard. She had her entire body on top of me, pushing down onto my body with all of her weight. I felt like I couldn't move and she was so heavy. I yelled, "Let me go, let go of me, you're hurting me!" But it was as if she couldn't hear a word I was saying. My words meant nothing. I was less than nothing to her. She was in such a rage she might not have even comprehended or understood my plea for release. I felt like she was on top of me for forever. Time had stopped. Her screams became louder, more obscene, and there was nobody to stop her. Her face turned red. As I stared at her face she started to look like the devil in human form. Her veins bulged from her forehead and her eyes bulged and took on a blank stare, a stare in which I was not viewed as a little girl, or even a human being, but a thing, a thing that was getting in the way of Misty's supposedly perfect life with my dad. I might as well have been a lifeless object. My hands and feet went numb; I began to lose circulation in my arms. I started to lose my strength. I just kept hoping that she would let me go. Somehow I eventually managed to get up and get away from her. As soon as I did, she chased after me. I immediately ran to the kitchen to get the cordless phone to call my mother. I ran as fast as I could around the other side of the house and back into my room and locked myself in there before she could get to me.

I tried to call my mom, but my hands were shaking so badly and I was in such a panic I couldn't remember my mother's phone number. Misty was now right outside my door, banging and screaming hysterically and demanding that I open it. Nothing was going to make me open that door, not after the torture I had just endured. I was going to stay locked in my room until my dad came home. 30 seconds later, the knocking stopped. I thought it was over, so I decided not call my mom, which would start another fight with my dad. That turned out to be a very bad decision.

All of a sudden I heard the doorknob turn; that crazy psycho had picked the lock! I hid behind the door and when the door opened and she walked in I shoved past her, ran out of my room and hid in the coat closet by the front door. I tried not to breathe or exist. I heard her go into the kitchen and bang a drawer shut. She began to call my name like we were in a twisted game of hide and seek. I was shaking and crying and trying to catch my breath and I just kept hoping that my dad would come home early. Her voice got closer and closer. I knew she had to be within a few feet of the closet door. Hiding in the closet seemed like a good decision in my frantic panic but now I was frightened that I would become trapped. If she found me, there would be nowhere for me to go. In that moment I made a quick decision, I would rather make my attempt at an escape, than be cornered in a dark closet. I pushed open the door out ran out. When I turned around she was standing right behind me with a large kitchen knife in her hand. I started crying loudly and told her that I was sorry, and that I didn't mean what I had written, and that I would throw the paper away. But it was too late.

She bolted towards me and I started running away from her as fast as I could. She started chasing after me with the knife in her hand. Was she trying to kill me? I was crying hysterically, I could barely catch my breath, my adrenaline was going, and I couldn't believe what was happening. I truly believed that I would have to defend myself and fight for my life. I ran into the kitchen and I grabbed the biggest knife I could find and turned to face her. Without thinking I rushed towards her with the knife and started to confront her. I ran after her and she started laughing as she began to run away from me. She thought it was funny. She was enjoying this. It was as if it was a sick game she was playing. A sick and evil game played with a helpless little girl. I don't know how, but I was able to get back to my room again, grabbed the cordless phone that was in my room and quickly dialed 911. I told the operator on the other end what had happened and she told me to stay on the phone with her but I needed to call my mom. I wanted a chance to tell my mom I loved her in case Misty got to me before help arrived. Immediately after I told the operator our address I hung up and I called my mom and tried to explain everything in 10 seconds what had happened and that she needed to come and get me. Once Misty realized I had called for help, I heard her go into the kitchen and quickly put her knife back in the drawer and then she yelled to me from the kitchen, "You are so dramatic Channon". She said this in such a calm adult voice. She was so good at being crazy. Then the chaos ended, or so I thought.

I stayed locked in my room, hiding under my bed with a million thoughts in my head of what was happening and what had occurred. I remained under the bed until my mom arrived. Not long after my mom arrived, the police showed up which created a huge scene in our neighborhood. I was so relieved knowing that I was now safe. Nothing would happen to me with other people around. Especially with the police or my mom near me. I was told to stay in my room while the police spoke to Misty and my mom. They both spoke to some of the officers outside to go over the story. I was scared I was going to get into trouble from my dad for calling the police on Misty but I didn't know what else to do. He still hadn't gotten home, but I knew he would find out what had happened. A little time went by and when the police were done talking to my mom and Misty, an officer came into my room to talk to me. The officer asked me to explain to him what had happened. I was so nervous to talk to the police.

I told them what had occured, and it seemed like everything was okay. The officers asked me to stay in my room, so I did. Thirty minutes later an ambulance arrived—I was then handcuffed and told that I would be put on a 72-hour 5150 hold in the hospital. I remained in handcuffs as they put me in the back of the ambulance. I didn't understand what was happening, I was so confused. I asked them what they were doing. I remember the officers kept saying that it was for my own safety. I thought to myself, my own safety? I wasn't the issue here, Misty was the problem and I was the victim. How did this get so turned around? I was freaking out, was I in trouble? I wanted my mom and dad. I didn't want to go to a hospital. I asked an officer if my mother could go with me and they said no. Misty had told the police that I had chased her around the house with a knife and tried to stab her. She said that I kept screaming and yelling that she broke my parents up and that I wanted her dead. Misty took the poem I wrote and showed it to the officers and my mom as proof that I hated her and made up stories. My poem, and Misty's made up story was enough to seal the deal with the police and enough evidence to have me taken away. She was such a good actress and so manipulative that she even convinced my own mother that she didn't do what she did. Soon after, the ambulance left with me in the back, handcuffed, and left to deal with every possible emotion a little girl could have. I was being ripped away from my home and I had no idea where I was being taken. I thought I was going to a regular hospital. I couldn't have been more wrong.

You never forget the first time you are committed to a psychiatric hospital. I was 12 years old. I remember it well. Frightened and terrified are a couple descriptions I would use. The name of the mental hospital was Pinegrove Psychiatric Hospital. I was admitted to the adolescent ward to be exact. I was in shock when I first arrived. Shocked and confused is a better way of putting it. I had never lied to my parents other than the occasional small lies kids often tell, like not eating a cookie before dinner kind of thing. So how did I end up here? Everything happened so fast and I couldn't understand why nobody believed me. Being taken into a mental hospital is fairly what you might imagine, something you would see in a movie, but nothing can prepare you for the feel of it all. It's as if it's not really happening but you keep waking up and realizing that it is real. The blank walls with no pictures, that smell that I just can't describe properly, the doctors in all white coats, the staff in scrubs, and the eerie quiet, yet random odd noises that creep into your ear. But before I could even comprehend my environment, there are standard procedures for newcomers. They took my shoelaces and my ponytail holder away. They also made me remove the drawstring from my pants that I was wearing at the time. Anything that could be used to hurt yourself or someone else was taken from me. I was given a pamphlet of my rights as a patient there. I had to keep asking myself over and over if this was real. I could not believe I was standing in an asylum. Every second was like a surreal nightmare that refused to end. I hoped that I would wake up. I could not stop crying, and all I wanted to do was go home.

After the initial check in a nurse walked me to my room, and as we walked, I passed by other kids that were much older than me. They all looked really messed up, and they were staring directly at me. It was a very scary feeling. Some kids looked like zombies; their eyes were all glazed over, like there was nothing behind them, those kids didn't look at you, they looked through you. One of the girls I walked past was openly drooling. I didn't belong there. I was freaking out. I kept asking questions like "How long am I going to be here? Can I call my mom? Why did you take my shoelaces?" The nurse did not say a word, or answer any of my questions she just ignored me as if I didn't matter anymore now that I was there. We kept walking down a long hallway until we finally came upon a room. Then she turned and said, "This is your room; a doctor will be by tomorrow to talk to you." That was it, no conversation, and no answers to my questions. The nurse was cold and distant, just like the room she had given me. Why was this happening to me? I was left in a room with white walls, no color, no art, no pictures, bars on the window, no mirrors in the bathroom, and no plants. There was no life whatsoever in that room. I sat on my bed in this hospital for the mentally ill, crying. I was completely alone, physically and emotionally. It was really cold, and I could not get warm. All I had with me was a tiny plastic toothbrush and a tiny tube of toothpaste, which the staff had given me when they checked me in. The mattress in my room was extremely uncomfortable and covered in thick plastic that made noise every time I turned on it. Everything was foreign, and I was completely on my own. I was homesick, and I missed my parents; I was so upset it made me feel sick to my stomach. I hoped all night my mom would arrive in panic and free me after they found out it was a big mistake. But nobody came to get me that night.

Something died inside of me in that hospital room right then and there. I don't know if it was my trust in people, or my parents, but I never saw the world the same way again. I cried myself to sleep that night, and a piece of my heart broke off. I would never be the innocent girl I once was. People were going to think I was crazy now. How would I explain this to my friends at school? My heart became hardened. That's when things started to change for the worse. I woke up the next morning to a room check, which is basically when the nurse comes in to check on you in case of suicide or misbehavior. It makes sense; because once you're in a place like that eventually it would make you want to kill yourself. At this point I was mentally exhausted. All night I had hoped someone would come and save me but it didn't happen. I had trouble sleeping, as you can imagine I heard screams throughout the night from other patients down the hall.

That morning I was very hesitant to leave my room. But I grew the courage to walk out of my room and down the empty hallways to an area that was like a living room where most of the other patients were in. When I walked into the room everyone stared at me. I was totally lost, I wasn't even sure I was allowed to leave my room and I didn't want to get in more trouble that I already in was at that point. I had no idea what I was doing. It made me extremely uncomfortable. I quietly sat down on a hard maroon couch and kept to myself. I was scared to talk to anyone. I wouldn't know what to say. I was embarrassed to even be there. I felt like a total outsider that got stuck in there by accident. I had a million thoughts racing through my head. Thoughts like, is one of these crazy kids going to try and attack me? What if no one likes me here? Am I ever going to get out of here? Will I be here forever? After awhile of sitting in silence with these crazy thoughts going through my head a girl came up to me and introduced herself. I was kind of glad someone was attempting to talk to me. Her name was Kirsty and she was also a patient there. She asked me what I was in for as if it was a prison. I told her in a very quiet voice because I didn't want anyone else to hear that I chased my stepmom around the house with a knife. She thought that was cool and we quickly became friends. She showed me the ropes in the ward about meal times, group therapy, everything I needed to know. Kirsty was in for trying to commit suicide, although she seemed totally normal to me. I was so glad to have met her because without her I would have been a lost sheep in that place. I don't know why, but I was never briefed on anything when I was first admitted to the mental hospital. They let you just figure it out as you go. Most of the other girls except Kirsty kept to themselves or were too drugged up to talk to. Others just looked like pure crazy and by that I mean their mind is in la la land. It is sad, but trust me, when you have to live in close quarters to those people you really want to stay away from them, they are bad news bears. I met with a psychiatrist that day in an office that was in our ward. It was a square room by the nurses station with nothing but two chairs in it. Nothing else was in the room. Psych wards are known to never have many objects in sight because they are afraid the patients will hurt themselves, or others with them.

He asked how I had slept and then asked that I explain what happened and how I ended up there. I tried to tell him it was a huge mistake and that I did not belong there. I asked when I would be able to go home and if I could call my mom and he basically avoided my questions and told me that visiting hours were only at certain times and phone calls weren't allowed until day 3. "Day 3!?" I asked. There was no way I was going to stay in there for three days, I could barely take one night in that god awful place. I was screaming on the inside. I felt trapped and my anxiety levels were going through the roof. He wasn't very friendly and was really starting to piss me off because I needed to get out of there! I was hopeful that once I met with him he would answer my questions and help me so I could go home, but the meeting was not going my way at all. He made me feel like I was not being truthful with him. Not even this doctor that was supposed to be helping me believed anything I said. Once I realized I wasn't leaving anytime soon and that he thought I was lying I got angry and lost it. I was starting to go crazy, literally. If you've never been to a psych ward let me explain what these places are like. You are forcefully thrown into a place similar to jail, but this is much worse than jail. I know because I have been there and will explain more on that later on in my story. They don't just lock you up and take you as a person out of society. They made me feel less human and if that wasn't bad enough then they slowly take your mind away as well. Fed up, and mad that this new doctor didn't believe me, I lost my sh★t. I started screaming, yelling and swearing at him that he needed to let me go and that I didn't belong there. It was a big mistake on my part. Once again, Misty's story seemed very valid to the doctor with me losing my temper. But I couldn't help it. He eventually calmed me down and after only 30 minutes of talking to me, he prescribed medication and had a diagnosis for me. He told me that I had what was called bi-polar disorder.

The doctor prescribed Lithium for me three times a day and Seroquel at night. He said it would keep me calm and help me sleep. I didn't want to take it, but he insisted. So I did. I didn't want to feel sad anymore, and he said the sadness would go away. Besides, he was a doctor so I trusted him. The next day, the pills started to take effect and I was a walking zombie, just like everyone else in there. I couldn't believe what was happening to me. I felt slow and my brain was foggy. I did not feel like myself, and I did not like the way it made me feel. I couldn't think straight. I lost motivation to do anything. I did not even care anymore if my parents came to visit or not.

Once the medicine was in my system I pretty much blacked out for most of my stay there which is the scariest part. I only recall bits and pieces of what actually happened to me and what they did to me and the other patients there. I had no idea how long I was even there, that's how bad I was drugged. One day Kirsty told me she had been hiding her meds in her gums. I had to take meds 3 times a day so I decided I would try and hide my lunchtime meds. When it came time and my name was called to take my meds I put them in my mouth and tried to hide the pill in my gums really fast but failed miserably. When they pass out meds in the hospitals they make you take the meds in front of the nurse and they check your mouth to make sure you actually took them. The nurse checked and saw I was trying to hide my meds. I was threatened with the "quiet room," but I thought it would be like a hospital time out, and at that point, I would rather take a time out than my meds. I told the nurse "You can't force me to take these drugs if I don't want them". She rolled her eyes, and said "Yes you do have to take them and if you don't we will have a problem". I responded back with, "F**k you!" I said it so loud I think everyone around heard me say it. The room grew quiet and I looked around at everyone in the room, they were all staring at me in disbelief at what I had just done. I couldn't believe that I had disrespected someone like that but something inside me had changed during my stay in that hospital. Suddenly, all the girls in the ward started screaming, clapping, banging their plastic green lunch trays on the tables, and throwing their food at the nurse. All hell broke loose because I had refused to take my meds and cussed at the nurse. Wow, this is kind of fun I thought to myself. I jumped on top of the lunchroom table and started dancing because I had just caused these miserable patients to smile and have fun in a place where no one ever smiles. Some of the other patients started dancing on the table with me and it was like a awesome psych patient party. That 2 minutes of fun was about to come to a quick halt. The nurse called in a code, and 15 seconds later three male nurses tackled me down to the ground and were trying to give me a shot in my butt. I kicked and screamed; I had no idea what they were trying to do to me but I was freaking out. No one told me about the shot, what it was for, or even what it was. I thought I was being attacked. All the girls in the ward started yelling "Booty juice! Booty juice!" In a psych ward, when one person goes nuts, everyone does, kind of like a domino effect. It's quite exciting, when you aren't the person getting in trouble. The nurses injected me with Klonopin, which is a powerful tranquilizer. The shot works instantly and I went from dancing on a table to kicking and screaming and then Jello-O in their arms.

They carried me off to the quiet room, which is a padded room like what you see in the movies, except not as nice, less bright, and much dirtier. Everything was getting really blurry and I felt as if I was coming in and out of it. The room they put me in smelled like death. I was then restrained to the bed. They had taken my clothes off, put me in a hospital gown and retrained my wrists and ankles in leather cuffs that were connected to a metal bed. I remember coming in and out of it and not even being able to itch my nose or scratch my arm. I kept screaming for someone to help me. I swear I screamed for someone to get me out of their for what felt like hours. I think they forgot about me because no one came to feed me or check on me at least that I can remember. I thought I was going to die in there. I couldn't move. I screamed for help but no one came. I screamed myself into exhaustion and it was the most torture I had ever endured aside from Misty's abuse. I think they gave me too big of a shot because I slept and was in and out for what felt like days. I woke up to a nurse helping me walk out of the quiet room to see my mom who had finally come to visit me. I was drooling a lot, could barely keep my eyes open, and couldn't put a sentence together. I had horrible bruises around my wrists and ankles from trying to get out of my restraints. I looked like an insane person. I looked worse than I did when I first went into the ward. My mother saw me and didn't even recognize me. When she realized I was her daughter she promptly demanded answers of why I couldn't walk or talk and why I looked the way I did. She was screaming at the nurses asking, " What the hell did you do to my daughter?!" The nurse explained, but my mother was livid. She checked me out of the ward the next day, thank God. I was so happy, and I thought to myself I will never go back to a place like that again. Wishful thinking on my part....too bad that wasn't the case.

THESE ARE THE LESSONS I LEARNED:

I am now petrified of psych wards. The main thing I learned from this experience is that there is no drug in the world that can replace real life and happiness. When you hand someone over to a psychiatrist, say goodbye. They may never return. Now, this is not true for everyone, but it was for me.

I learned one fundamental thing through that experience. As a child, you do not have much control over what happens to you. I was put into a psych ward against my will. But what you do have control over is how you choose to experience what you go through and the way that you think and perceive things. You could think like I did, "life as I know it is over," or you can change the way you think about the whole situation. If I could have written a letter to my twelve-year-old self, it would have read: Channon, this sucks! But there is always someone else that is worse off than you—be grateful for what you do have that is positive, and no matter how bad something is, it could be worse! At least you are in a safer place where Misty cannot hurt you. You are still alive. You won't be in here forever. Think about the things you are grateful for instead of all the bad things going on, and you will be on your way to true happiness. It is during the worst times in our lives that we need to change the way we think about our experiences.

Chapter 4

I Hate You – Don't Leave Me: Childhood Bipolar Disorder

*"Great spirits have often encountered
violent opposition from weak minds."*

ALBERT EINSTEIN

The psychiatrist had told my mother that I was bi-polar and that I would not be able to live a normal life without medication. I was prescribed 500mg of Lithium three times a day and Seroquel once in the morning and once at night before bed. The decision to put me on that medicine ended up being a serious mistake and the beginning of a serious downhill path for me. The meds prescribed to me were to control my bi-polar disorder. I was so frustrated with everything going on and I had lost a big part of my soul in that hospital. Because of all of that, I became very rebellious—and I was on heavy psychiatric medication as well, not a great combination.

During those 30 minutes of meeting me, the psychiatrist "diagnosed" me with this serious disorder, no test needed. Oh yes, and my behavior as observed in the hospital contributed to the doctor's conclusion of my mental state. Well, I can tell you that nobody acts like their normal self when thrown into a mental asylum. One man's opinion would send me on a journey that nearly ended my life so many times. I was still coming to the reality that my parents put me in a psych ward, and now I had to take this brain altering medication. It was a lot for me to handle. My parents made sure I took every single pill the doctors said I needed. The doctor had scared us into thinking that if I did not take it, something terrible would happen. We were told I would hurt my family or myself! Being young, I believed what the doctor said and what my parents told me to do. I believed all of it. I didn't know any better at the time.

I was placed in an outpatient therapy program by the state called the Family and Child Guidance Center and saw a therapist twice a week to talk about my feelings. I hated it. I didn't want to talk about all the horrible things happening in my life, I wanted to forget them. Naturally, therapists want you to open up and talk about your problems. I did the opposite and would just be quiet and not talk at all. This really annoyed my therapist when I went in for our meetings and didn't say a word. I was extremely defiant and no longer respected or trusted my elders. I did this for awhile until one day she took out art supplies during our session and said if I didn't want to talk I could paint or draw my feelings. The idea of art and painting caught my attention and it was finally something I was up for. So I ended up painting in therapy and it actually did make me feel better. Ever since that day I have always used art as my outlet for when I can't explain what I am feeling or to make myself feel better. As I got older, I would write songs, do art, and now—write books. It's a creative outlet I have always needed and used to express myself in ways I wouldn't otherwise know how. During the time I was in outpatient therapy, my parents were given a book on bi-polar disorder to help them better understand my supposed mental illness, but neither of them read it. If they weren't going to try and understand my illness, then why should I try and learn more about it? Maybe if we would have read it and educated ourselves more on it, maybe they could help me and wouldn't keep sending me to everyone else to fix me. After all, I was doing all these things for their attention.

One day I was extremely agitated in a therapy session. I really did not want to be there. All my friends were hanging out and seeing a movie and I couldn't go because I had to go to stupid therapy. I was not getting better and therapy was not helping. I was pissed that I had to be there that day and was throwing some major attitude to my therapist. She was not having it and ended up yelling at me in the session. I freaked out and threatened to kill her if she tried yelling at me again like that. She immediately walked out of the room and left me in there by myself. I didn't know if she was scared of me, or going to talk to my mother. Next thing I know I have my therapist walking back in with a security officer. He stood there in the room and I looked at her and said, "Really? You brought in a rent a cop?" She said, "Channon you can't threaten to kill people, that will land you back in the hospital." As soon as she said that, it set off a major trigger for me and I went ape sh*t crazy in her office. I picked up my chair and threw it at her. I started screaming telling her to not threaten me, just crazy stuff really. I think whatever meds they had me on really put me on edge and made me way crazier than I already was at the time. I tried to stab the security officer with a pen that was sitting on my therapist's desk. He ended up restraining me with handcuffs but not after a serious struggle. I put up a good fight. I had turned into a mental patient that everyone was trying to help get better but I was only getting worse, much worse. I went back to the mental hospital again that day, and had been admitted to the psych ward seven different times that same year.

Fast forward a few months and I was admitted to the psych ward again, but this time Misty would be coming with me. Misty did everything for my dad, she waited on him hand and foot. That disturbed woman worshipped him like a god, and her obsession over him was not healthy. I never did believe that she loved him. Why would she intentionally hurt him and his kids if she loved him? Misty was a sick psychopath.

One evening during dinner Misty poked me with a fork at the dinner table because my elbows were on the table—it was rude to do that you see. I didn't get a warning, or a verbal request, just a poke with a fork into my elbow. My father saw it, and asked her not to do that again. But being 13 years old and on meds, I forgot shortly afterwards, and my elbows popped back onto the table. Misty stabbed me with the fork again in the same place on my elbow, but this time breaking my skin and causing me to bleed. My father witnessed it again, and this time he was angry. I would have punched that crazy b★tch in the face if my dad wasn't already reprimanding her. He yelled at Misty, which caused her to freak out. She started cussing and saying that I had no manners and that someone needed to teach me because nobody else was going to because he was never around. My father told her that is not how you punish children, and especially not his. My dad stuck up for me that night, and then proceeded to talk about how her kids had worse manners and it ended up a heated argument that lasted about an hour. I was just so happy that my dad had seen what happened and stood up for me. It made me feel like he actually did love me, and that he cared about me.

My dad didn't talk to Misty for the rest of the night and I could visibly see that she was upset and really distraught by it. I didn't know it at the time, but I guess Misty was so upset that she took some pills and started drinking that night. Later that night after everyone had gone to sleep, Misty quietly came into my room. My room had its own bathroom and was on the other side of the house. She came in, turned my light on which woke me up, and locked my door. I wasn't sure why she was waking me up but I thought maybe she had come to apologize for what had happened earlier that night at the dinner table. I thought if she was actually here to apologize, she's only here to try and make things better with my dad and not me. Either way, I was annoyed, and I had school the next day so I wasn't happy that I was woken up. I was barely awake and my Seroquel meds were completely kicked in so I was kind of out of it. She told me she wanted to talk to me. I slowly sat up on my bed and then she asked me to go into the bathroom with her. I thought it was weird but I did it anyways because I was half asleep. As we entered my bathroom, she locked the door behind us.

Once the lock clicked, I realized she had me exactly where she wanted me. Misty was out of it too and was acting very strange. I could see her eyes were glazed over. I'd seen a look similar to this with her before, but this time her eyes took on the feeling of methodical planned intent of harm. I sensed something bad was going to happen, and immediately grew nervous and I had reason to be. Within seconds, she tackled me down and sat on top of me. Just as before, pinning me down. I was helpless yet again and under the weight of this crazy psycho. She began kissing and licking me all over my face. I was so disgusted I wanted to throw up. She said if my father wasn't going to kiss her goodnight, then I would have to. I asked her nicely to get off me. It was a good thing I was heavily medicated because at this point of my life I would have tried to kill her. My arms started tingling. Then they started to go numb. I was trapped and restrained, underneath her. I kept asking her over and over to leave me alone but she just ignored me. She had something else in mind. Instead, she reached for something in the pocket of the robe she was wearing. As her hand went into her pocket, she told me that it was all my fault that my dad was mad at her and not talking to her. She said that I was going to pay for making it all happen. I could barely make out her words, she was slurring and started mumbling other things I couldn't make out. She was basically talking crazy. By this time I was terrified, and as I looked over towards her pocket, I watched her pull out a razor blade. She took the razor blade and began to cut the inside of my wrists. I think I went into shock or took myself into another place mentally because I don't remember screaming or shouting—I just let it happen. As the blade sliced my wrists, she mumbled a bunch of stuff I still could not understand. It was like everything went quiet. "What are you doing? Will you please get off of me, you're scaring me!" I knew I was talking but I couldn't hear myself, I had gone deaf. I started to struggle but I was trapped under her weight and could not move. I started panicking. I slowly started to hear sound again and then she said, "This time you are going away for a long time. Hopefully you will never come back. I can't have bitchy red troublemakers like you coming between me and love. I can't believe the nerve you have to cause a fight between us. You do it on purpose don't you?" She kept saying red, red, red over and over again. All I could think in my head was, 'you crazy psychopath when I get up I am going to kill you'. She started cutting me with passion, as if she loved the feeling it gave her. She drove the razor blade deeper and faster into my wrists as tears fell down my face. She started laughing as she cut me. She watched in awe as my blood dripped off of my arms. Suddenly my wrists hurt badly and blood was everywhere. I think at this stage reality set in for me and I started to come out of the initial shock of what was happening.

It was then I realized I didn't think she was trying to kill me; she just wanted to hurt me and see me suffer as she did earlier that night. She was getting pure enjoyment from torturing me. She liked watching me in pain. She cut both my arms over and over. Both of my arms were cut from my elbows to my wrists. In the moment I thought well at least there is no way she will be able to get away with this, there is physical proof of what she's done to me! It all happened so fast and as soon as she was done, she quickly climbed off me and threw the razor blade in my sink. Misty ran off into the kitchen where I heard her wash her hands, pour herself another drink, and I also heard the sounds of a pill bottle.

I had no clue what she was doing, but I wasn't about to wait around any longer to find out. I ran across the other side of the house into my dad's room and woke him up. I showed him my bloody wrists and told him Misty had cut me and I started to explain the story. My dad jumped out of bed to confront Misty but when he came out, she was lying on the floor of the kitchen passed out. She must have overdosed on pills or passed out from too much alcohol. I thought she was just faking it. But then I heard police sirens growing closer to our house. At some point, Misty had already called the hospital or police or something before passing out, because the police and ambulance arrived before we even had the chance to call them ourselves. When the ambulance arrived my father did not know what to say, as my wrist cuts looked like suicide cuts. I would never have cut myself, nor at the time did I even know how to. I told the emergency staff I did not do it, that Misty had, but she was out cold. Again—neither my dad nor the ambulance staff believed me. Nobody believed me, even with the incident that my father witnessed at the table I was still on my own, and once again I was off to an asylum for something I never did. I could not trust a single soul. I had no one to confide in, nobody to listen to me. The last place I wanted to go was to the hospital again. I had already been there so many times already, I knew how awful those places were. I kept crying and saying, "No, no, please no, please I don't want to go back there." This time they were sending me to UCLA Psychiatric Hospital. However, Misty would be joining me the next day. She had taken so many pills and drank so much alcohol she needed to have her stomach pumped. I'm still not sure if she had taken the pills and alcohol in an attempt for my dad's attention, or to try and cover her tracks by passing out in an attempt to prove she wasn't available to harm me at the time, or if she was going to try and say I hurt her and then tried to kill myself, who knows. As smart as her attempts were, it only worked half way. Sure she got me sent away, but at the same time, she screwed herself in the process.

Thankfully, the adult ward and the adolescent ward are separate. It was a good thing too, because I really did want to kill her. I was in pain from the cuts, my arms were sore, and once again she had landed me in another scary place. Another asylum. How was she able to get away with all of this? She knew that since I had already been in mental hospitals and diagnosed as bi-polar, getting me back in another ward would be easy. Once people find out you have a mental disorder or that you've been to a mental hospital, it's easy to judge and dismiss you. People tend to automatically think you are crazy. It sucks, so if you get misdiagnosed, or sent to a psychiatric hospital by accident or mistake, it's hard to break away from that stigma. Your notes and records are all kept on file. Good luck breaking free from all of that. I was upset, mad, pissed off, angry, hurt, sad, every negative emotion you could think of. Could I do anything about it though? No.

Being in another psych ward sucked, but this place was bigger and nicer than Pinegrove or Northridge Hospital. It didn't have such a negative feel, but then again this wasn't my first time around. Maybe I sort of knew what to expect. UCLA had art therapy twice a week, which was nice. I could paint and make candles! Even though I hated being there, I was safe from Misty. I knew she couldn't hurt me when I was locked away in these places. I met a few other girls who had it rough at home, so I didn't feel so alone. UCLA is a teaching hospital and the doctors moved around in packs. So there were 8 doctors who would come and see me. These doctors thought I should change from Lithium to Depakote in higher doses to see how I would react on them. I felt like a science experiment. I hated the drugs they were giving me but I usually took them anyway. Sometimes if I could hide them and not take them I would, and other days I just didn't care and would take them as they requested.

I had spent so much time in mental hospitals at this point that I was getting better at hiding my meds. But I will say this, no matter how many times you've been sent to an insane asylum it never gets easier. They suck just as much as the first time. Sometimes it would get so bad in there and I just couldn't take being locked away another second that I would purposely act out to get "booty juice" so some of my stay was slept away with the help of the drugs. Then I would kick myself because it just made me have to stay there even longer. I would go so crazy in the hospital I would sit on the cold ground in the corner and rock myself back and forth to pass the time. I hadn't realized it then but I had turned into one of the girls that I was scared of when I walked into my first mental hospital. My mind and soul had been stripped away from me by the amount of drugs that were being given to me on a daily basis by the doctors. When you are bad, or act out, they just sedate you enough so that you can't really do anything.

A few days later, my mom came to visit with my Aunt Jen. I was so happy when my family would visit me and I looked forward to it more than anything. I started to get used to hospital life and it began to feel like my second home. My time at the UCLA ward just went by as usual I guess you could say. For some reason I don't have as vivid of a memory of UCLA as I did at Pinegrove. Maybe it was the meds, or maybe I just was getting better at blocking stuff out of my memory.

I was released from the UCLA hospital just before turning 14 years old and just before I was about to go into 7th grade. It was time for a new school, middle school. None of my friends were going to my middle school, so it was a clean slate in a new private school.

(In Order: Khloe Kardashian, Me, Ashley, and Danny on our way to a field trip)

Montclair College Prep was expensive and prestigious, and I was accepted there on a sports scholarship. I made some new friends there and I also made friends with now celebrity Khloe Kardashian. Khloe was super sweet to me. We were good friends and hung out all the time.

She wasn't famous back then although her stepdad dad was a professional athlete and I remember her showing me a Wheaties box with his face on it in their kitchen one day when I went over to her house after school. I didn't really think that much about it, and I knew where they lived there were other celebrities but it wasn't of any importance to me. Almost every kid's parents at that school were famous or rich for something. Khloe was cool, and all that I remember was that I wanted for her to teach me how she did her amazing make-up; she was so good at it.

There were a lot of celebrity kids at that school. I really enjoyed it but I often felt like the poor kid there on a scholarship, but it was a top-notch school and everyone was really nice so it didn't matter.

I even got my first boyfriend at that school. His name was Danny; he was blonde with blue eyes, and had a great smile. We only kissed on the lips a few times, but back then of course it was a lot for me and a pretty grown up thing to do! There were a lot of boys that liked me and I thought it was really cool, especially since I thought I was hideous and fat. Another good friend I made at the time was Ashley. She was a total rebel and had very wealthy parents like most of the kids at school. One day after school we went to her house and I realized that she also had a workaholic father who was absent from her life. It was a huge thing we could both relate to each other on. Ashley lived next door to a Playboy model and would go over there and hang out and get to try on all of her sexy clothes. I remember going over to the Playboy model's house and seeing how cool it was. I was fascinated by her lifestyle. Her house was decorated so awesome and she had so many amazing things I had never seen before like a couch in the shape of lips! Everything was so modern and expensive looking. It was so much fun hanging out with her. The home itself was gorgeous, and I could tell she had a lot of money. The Playboy model was blonde, beautiful, and really cool. One day she told us she was going to Vegas and Ashley asked her if we could go with her. She laughed and said if it was okay with our parents, sure. I don't think the model thought Ashley's dad would actually say yes. We were only 14 years old! But we wanted to go so badly. We begged and eventually convinced Ashley's dad to let us go. He had been drinking so it really could have gone either way, but to our surprise he let us go! Besides, rich kids always get what they want. We were so excited. Going to Vegas with a Playboy model at the age of 14, who get's to do that? I had never been to Vegas before. I couldn't believe how cool it was. I was in awe when we got there. We were staying at a really nice hotel. We even had our own room that was directly connected to the model's room.

The Playboy model invited some friends over and then they all went out for the night, so we snuck into her room to check it out. There was cocaine on the tables and all kinds of party stuff I wasn't used to seeing. There was also a pack of cigarettes. Ashley and I were too scared to get caught stealing from the model, so we left all of it alone. Instead, we hung around in the hallways of this fancy hotel and stole half smoked cigarettes from hall ashtrays by the elevators, which we brought back to our hotel room. We found some matches and both tried cigarettes for the first time. They were so nasty, but we thought we were so cool. After all, we were only 14 years old and in Vegas by ourselves practically. It was probably the coolest thing I had ever done in my life.

After the Vegas trip, another girl from school invited me to a slumber party, just the two of us. Her name was Brogan. We stole a whole pack of cigarettes from her mom's carton in the freezer and each smoked four cigarettes in the attic that night. She let me keep a few and I hid some cigarettes in my eyeglasses case, and at the age of 14 I started smoking consistently. Brogan also did something weird that night—she asked me if I wanted to watch her make out with her dog. I told her I didn't really want to see that but she did it anyway. It was one of the weirdest things I had seen. One thing I learned at that school is rich kids do some weird sh★t, and by rich I mean filthy rich. The next day at school I was in the locker room changing for basketball practice and she came in screaming and yelling asking me if I had told people that she made out with her dog. I said yes and then she instantly punched me in the face. I was kind of shocked but there were a bunch of other girls in the locker room and I didn't want to look like a little b★tch so I hit her back and then a huge fight broke out in the locker room. I kicked her a$$. She got detention, and I was expelled from school. I wasn't even the one that started the fight, but I was on a scholarship so the blame was put on me. Besides, money buys everything and my parents didn't have enough money to pay off the principle to keep me there. Once I was expelled, my parents were pissed and decided to put me into a public school for the first time. I was used to private schools and smaller classrooms. We were already three months into the school year so I was really scared to start a new school, and a public school instead of a private one. No more private schools for me after that incident. My parents were so upset with me and I had let them down.

This is me in junior high, you can tell in my face my weight gain, and FYI for everyone who thinks my lips are fake, this picture should prove to you all that I naturally have big lips and I have only had them done 2 times and they are natural now

My new public school was overcrowded and dirty and I did not want to be there. I hated having to be the new girl at school all the time and not knowing anyone, it is very awkward. The medication I had been taking made me gain a few pounds, so I was overweight for the first time in my life.

My eating disorder started to become worse because of it. I wouldn't eat in front of anyone. It made me feel bad to eat, and I would throw up all of my food at school and at home. The girls in that school were pretty and skinny, and I was ugly and fat. Misty was also a great reminder of my weight and looks. I got in trouble at school a lot, and my mom wasn't around much because she was always working. Sometimes I didn't go to school at all. It felt good to be bad. I hated my new school, I think mostly because I hated myself and because I didn't really fit in there. All the girls had there own groups they were in and I was the outcast and the new girl.

My mother had no idea that I was skipping school or that I was getting into trouble at school. She came home so late that I was able to delete the messages on our home phone from the school before she ever got to hear them. My eating disorder spun out of control too. I lost a lot of weight, and my mom began to notice. After a few weeks of noticing, she sat me down and I told her what had been happening. She said I had to go to see our primary care doctor. The doctor said I was very thin and if I didn't start eating that I could die. My mother was very upset. She started crying in the office and said she would do anything if I started eating again. I told her that I wanted to get my belly button pierced, and that if she took me to get it pierced, I would eat a cheeseburger from McDonald's. So we went straight from the doctor's office to the tattoo parlor. I got my belly button pierced, and I felt so cool. I would be the only girl at my school with a pierced belly button and having my belly button pierced would make me a lot more popular at my new school. After my piercing, we headed to McDonald's and I ate my cheeseburger, but anyone with an eating disorder will tell you that it does not just go away. I just became better at hiding it from my mother. I hated the guilt I would get from eating, and I tried to drink as little water as possible to prevent any water weight. This went on for awhile until one morning I felt so ill and I couldn't get out of bed. When I tried, I collapsed onto the floor. Starvation had taken its toll, and I was nothing but skin and bones. I was dizzy and had depleted myself of food, water, and nutrients for too long. My mom could not miss work, so she called my therapist to deal with me. Once again, I was admitted to UCLA, but I was admitted to a section of the hospital for people with eating disorders. I wish my mother had been there more often and spent more time with me instead of always sending me off to a professional to deal with my teenage problems. I think we could have worked on my different problems together if she would have made the time. I know she loves me, and it was difficult for both of us, but I guess I would have felt more loved if I wasn't passed along to the next doctor all the time. I don't know if I was doing some things for attention or if I was just truly unhappy. Either way, I know it wasn't right of me, but at the time the only way I received attention was by doing something drastic. The eating disorder unit was a very depressing place. The bathrooms at the hospital remained locked, it smelled awful in there like a rotting smell and you could only use them a few hours after eating. That way your food had enough time to digest and you would not be able to throw it up. The staff would watch you eat, and basically force you to eat. I hated that place with a passion. There was no adolescent ward in the ED rehab facility and it was mainly older women so it was weird for me being the youngest patient. I finally made it out of there and I was so happy when I left that place that smelled like rotting people. After I left it was a struggle and I tried hard to get better and slowly but surely I did.

I got back into the swing of school as I was away for awhile. All the kids at school thought I was crazy, and it was true, I was. As soon as I thought everything was going well another problem arose. I couldn't stand one of my teachers at my new school and I mouthed off to her one day in class. I started to leave her class in the middle of a lecture to go have a cigarette, and the teacher stopped talking and tried to stop me from leaving class. She asked, "Where are you going?" I responded, "I am leaving, I can't understand a word you say and I am not learning anything in your class, so I am leaving to go smoke a cigarette outside." My honesty has always gotten me in trouble and it still does. My teacher was pissed and basically told me in a very firm voice to sit down and that I wasn't allowed to leave. I had serious problems with authority figures telling me what to do so I told her to go f^$@ herself and I walked out. It ended up causing a huge ordeal and the principal was called. To be honest, I really didn't care if I was going to get in trouble, in fact it didn't feel normal for me to not be in trouble. The principal found me 15 minutes later and told me that I was not allowed to smoke on campus so I told her I would leave campus and go home, which is exactly what I did. I walked home and the next day I was expelled.

Needless to say my mom was pissed and disappointed yet again and had to find me another school to attend, bless her heart. This was my third school in one year! Guess what happened? I got expelled from that school too! At least I can add some humor in my story and say that I got expelled for different reasons at each school. Let me explain though, within less than a month at my new school, I found some diet pills in my mother's house and started taking them to speed up my metabolism and to lose weight. A girl I had met at my new school wanted to buy some from me, so I sold her a whole bunch of them. A few days later I found out that girl ended up overdosing on them. When she was in the hospital her parents asked her where and whom she got the pills from and she had blamed me for selling her "drugs" on campus. Obviously, I got in big trouble for that which was why I was expelled again from another school.

I was on so many medications and was getting into more trouble than ever before. I did not care about much or life at all, but I knew that if I screwed up at the next school, I would be held back a grade.

I hated school and couldn't wait till I didn't have to go anymore so I did not want to get held back. My fourth school was tough; I did not know anyone and I did not understand anything because of the constant switching of schools. I was so lost in every class and I couldn't catch up. I was lonely, miserable, and had no friends. I was always the crazy new girl at school that everyone was talking about behind my back. It was a good thing we lived in Los Angeles and had a ton of different schools to put me into.

Every day I became more and more depressed. The kids made fun of my clubbed thumbs, a condition that you are born with. It's a condition where the tips of your thumbs are shorter than normal. I started hiding my thumbs in my sweaters because they embarrassed me. I was really unhappy in middle school, and there were times when I felt so low and like such a failure that I wanted to kill myself. My life was awful, my parents hated me, and I didn't have any friends because I couldn't stay in school long enough to make any so I was just miserable. I felt bad for my parents having to deal with me. I felt like no one would care if I died, and that they didn't love me anyway. No one would miss me and their lives would be easier without me in it. I felt this way for months and I felt this feeling of being so empty and lost and that I was never going to be anybody or amount to anything. Everything Misty had said about me was true. I was exhausted from life and feeling this way, and decided I wanted to end my life. Another day of this shitty life I was living was too much for me to handle. I couldn't stand another day of feeling so depressed. I was going to commit suicide. I sat in class and started planning in my head how I would end my life. I couldn't stop crying thinking about it; I just kept wiping away my tears in class staying really quiet so no one would notice me crying. I didn't want to cut my wrists, because I wouldn't want my mom to have to clean that up and I wouldn't want my little sister to have to see that. After going through a bunch of scenarios in my head, I figured that the best way for me to end my life was to overdose on my Seroquel pills. My mom had just refilled my prescription at the pharmacy so I knew I had a full bottle of pills.

My Seroquel was a very strong medication. As soon as I took one of those pills at night, I would fall asleep in my dinner plate. So I figured if I took half the bottle, it would just put me to sleep and I would die peacefully. I realized that my mom would find me dead, but at least she would find me in my bed and it would look like I was sleeping. People seem to think that suicide is a selfish act but what they don't understand is how much pain we have to go through every second of our lives. How is that fair to us? The only way I can describe how it feels to want to kill yourself is how someone feels when they are dying of cancer, they are in pain constantly, emotionally and physically. They have a hard time getting out of bed, and they are sick all the time. That is what it feels like to be so severely depressed. It is almost impossible to want to stay alive. We just want to end the pain and suffering. You will never know what it feels like or be able to understand it unless you have been in that situation yourself. I had it all planned out. When I got home from school that day, I went straight to the kitchen where we kept my pills, grabbed the whole bottle, and went immediately to my bathroom upstairs. As I entered my bathroom I stared at myself in the mirror for awhile. It was quiet, as if I tuned everything else out. I watched the tears stream down my face. Then I fixed my hair, I wanted to look pretty when they found me. I saw the pain behind my eyes, the hurt, the regret, and the loss of everything bright and happy in my life. I didn't want to live like this anymore. I couldn't do it anymore. The pain and suffering was too much to take. If this was what my life had truly become, then I would give it up. I would rather be dead than live another day in my life. I slowly opened the plastic orange prescription pill bottle of Seroquel and poured the pills into my hand. And just like that, I just started taking five pills at a time until half the bottle was gone.

Here is what I learned:

- If you are severely depressed, you need to seek help whether it's from a therapist, parent, family member, or friend. I know it can be hard to tell someone how you truly feel inside and you may think no one cares, but life is meant to be happy and fun, and no one wants to feel sad. Also, know that a therapist can only help you help yourself. You have to want to get better in order to get where you want to be.

- I was in a period of my life when I was dealing with so many different things: an eating disorder, being bullied at school, depression, bi-polar disorder and feeing abandoned by my parents. Now I know that I was starving for attention and I wanted someone to care about me, so I acted out and did all these things I knew were wrong, but at the end of the day, I hurt myself the most.

- Do not ditch school no matter how boring or awful it may be to you; go to school, and pay attention. When you grow up, you will need to be educated to get a decent job. You want to have a nice house, right? A cool car? A good job? Well, you will not get that nice life unless you stay in school! Also, it is really embarrassing when you do not know the answer to easy questions—take it from me.

- Have you ever heard the saying "you are who your friends are"? It is so important to find the right friends. I have had friends who were very mean to me. I wish I would have had the courage to stop being friends with them. People that are mean to you do not deserve to have you as their friend. Most of the time when someone says or does hurtful things to you it is because they are hurt themselves and they want to bring you down to their level. It is not you, it is them, misery loves company.

Chapter 5

Cutting Out the Pain

*Everything happens for a reason and
works out for the best in the end.*

JOY ROSE

Committing suicide doesn't always come easy. Especially when you've chosen a way to die that doesn't happen instantly. Pills take time to do their job. So what do you do in the meantime? What do you think about? Well, unfortunately, and fortunately, you have time to think of everything imaginable. As soon as I swallowed all those pills I started to get a little scared. It's difficult to really comprehend death and an ending to life, especially at such a young age. I started to think what if I did not die peacefully? What if I start feeling really sick? I started to panic, and then I was able to calm myself down, only to find myself back to the reality of standing in my bathroom staring at myself in the mirror crying and wondering what I had just done. I wanted to die, but at the same time I didn't. I started to feel a small sense of regret come over me, which then turned into a huge overwhelming feeling of regret. In addition, I started to feel really strange. My face turned from a flushed red color to pale white then grey and I started to get very light headed. It was difficult to tell how much time had already passed, so I wasn't sure if I started to have a panic attack or if the pills had enough time to kick in and were slowly starting to kill me. I didn't know, but at that moment I knew I didn't want to die anymore. I rushed to grab the phone and I frantically called my mom at work and told her what I had done. I could barely breathe at this stage. I started hyperventilating. The meds were definitely taking affect by this time. I didn't know if I would be able to control this and stay awake long enough to help myself or have someone save me.

My mom was mad, I could hear it in her voice but I needed her help more than anything right now. She said to stick my fingers down my throat and try to throw up the pills. I tried but nothing came up. I hadn't eaten much that day, so there was nothing to throw up. I was finally able to throw up just a little bit, but not much, not enough to make a difference. I don't remember much after that, the pills were doing their job as I had initially intended and they were taking my life away. Sometime later, the fire department broke down our apartment door. I wasn't awake or coherent during this time. This was all information I received after the fact. Apparently my mom had dialed 911 after I called her and the fire department found me and rushed me to the hospital. In the emergency room they pumped my stomach, and when I came to, they made me drink charcoal—it tastes disgusting. I kept telling the nurses I didn't want to die. Every time I woke up, I went into a panic attack. I remember grabbing the nurses' arms and squeezing them so tightly so they couldn't leave my side. I was panicked that I would die alone. My mom worked far from where we lived, and traffic in Los Angeles doesn't care if your child is sick.

I stayed overnight for observation. The next morning the doctors told me that with the amount of Seroquel in my body, they were surprised I was still alive and told me I was very lucky. My mom was so disappointed in me but she stayed with me in the hospital that night and told me how much she loved me and how sad she would be if I were dead. That was what I needed to hear, how come she never told me that before? We spoke that night in the hospital about seeing another psychiatrist because the medication I was on clearly was not helping at all. I was placed on a 72-hour 5150 hold in Northridge hospital but got out early because this time I knew what they wanted to hear to let me go. Mental hospitals were something I knew well by this time so I knew how to play the game and work the system. Life moved forward after those incidents and I was now in the 8th grade. I almost couldn't believe that I had passed 7th grade with everything that had happened during that year. I had been expelled from so many different schools in one year and hospitalized more than any other child the doctors had seen during that time.

I now had a new psychiatrist, who had taken me off Depakote and put me on Prozac.

We were told that it would take around three days for the new medication to settle in my system. I was very adamant about not taking these new drugs. I hated the way the medication made me feel, and I felt that I really did not need it. I remember begging my mother and doctor to let me try being on nothing for a while, but my psychiatrist was insistent. I needed medication we were told, or I would become suicidal again. I finally agreed to take the medication after he said I should try it for a week and see how it went.

Before leaving the doctor's office, I took my first Prozac pill. The next morning I felt like I was gone. Physically and mentally I just wasn't there, I wasn't present in life. I couldn't talk, I wouldn't talk, and I didn't even have thoughts running through my mind. I was almost convinced that I was a ghost and that I was successful with my suicide and this is what it felt like to be dead. The Prozac had stripped away my inner thoughts and feelings. My head felt like it was just floating around. The thoughts that once came naturally were now replaced by empty space. I existed with nothing: no thoughts, no needs, no desires, and no feelings of any kind. It wiped them all away. My mother would talk to me, and I would not hear her or even acknowledge that she was there.

Because the medication took away all feelings, I could not get angry or happy. Instead, I was just sad. I was sad without any reason because the medication had taken all of those reasons away. It just made me okay with hopelessness. The medication had the opposite effect on me that it was designed to have. But as the doctor said, it took time to work properly.

By the second day on my Prozac, things got really weird. Not only was I not talking, I was not eating, and I began to do very odd things. I would walk aimlessly around the house at a very slow pace and I would sit in the corner for hours staring at the wall. My mother even started to worry and took notice, but according to my excellent doctor, this was "normal" as it took three days for my body to adjust. The fact that my mom and sister were now scared of me, and that they stopped talking to me or being around me should have clued them into a serious problem with these meds. I was messed up though and don't blame them for not wanting to be around me.

On the third day, hopes were high that the medication would magically "level out" and suddenly solve all of my problems. The medication did not help me at all. It did the opposite and made me crazier as almost every kind of psychiatric medication does to people who are given the wrong kind of meds. I hadn't spoken in three days now and I was like a zombie. By the third day I was walking around the house at an extremely slow pace and I started to do something very strange. I started taking all the family pictures off the walls. My mom and sister were so scared of me at this point that they just let me do it.

By nighttime, I had locked myself in my room upstairs in my mom's 3-bedroom townhouse. That night my mother was in the kitchen doing dishes when she started to hear loud noises coming from my bedroom and outside the house. She finally went outside to see where all the noise was coming from. When she looked outside, she found all of my bedroom furniture, clothes, and belongings scattered on the ground in front of the house. It was like the aftermath of a tornado my mom had said. I had thrown every single object that I owned in my room out of my window from the second floor for no apparent reason. I had gone insane.

She ran upstairs to check on me and see what was going on. After banging on my door for awhile, I apparently calmly opened the door and looked straight past her. She yelled at me, but I didn't hear anything she said. It was as if she wasn't there. I slowly shut the door in her face. My mom quickly opened it back up before the door had shut all the way to continue yelling at me, but I continued to ignore her and looked right through her as though she was a ghost. Then I took a step towards her. She backed away, afraid. My sister heard the yelling and ran upstairs to see what was happening. I continued towards my mother, and when we reached the top of the stairs, I pushed her. She fell down two flights of stairs. She tumbled all the way down, her body twisting and limbs flying all which ways. I could have killed her that night. She laid at the bottom of the stairs

73

and cried. My mom was never one to cry, but she did that night. I do not know if she was crying from the fall, or because of what I had turned into, or both. The worst part was that I was not even slightly fazed by it.

Even if I had killed my mother that night, I would have felt nothing. I did not care if she was all right or not. I had no feelings of remorse or guilt, no shock, no increase in pulse. I was as calm as could be. I slowly walked back to my room and shut the door. My little sister called 911, and the police showed up around seven minutes later. I remember hearing walkie-talkies and people talking down stairs but in my mind it was as if I was hearing everything on TV. It didn't seem like it was all actually happening. When the police officers opened my door, he was met with a shocking sight. I had covered every square inch of my white walls in my now emptied out room with disturbing writing and drawings. No one even believed it was possible to draw so much in under 10 minutes time. The officers' report described an eerie energy, an empty room filled with death threats to therapists, doctors, teachers and family members, and also drawings of mutilated babies and people. I had used a box of crayons, and not one crayon nub remained. It took seven police officers to restrain me that night. I was biting them, kicking them, spitting on them, speaking gibberish and it was as if I had turned into a completely different person. I was a monster. I would have been scared of myself. My own family was deathly afraid of me and they had every right to be. Adrenaline is a deeply powerful thing. When it takes 7 police officers to restrain a one hundred and fifteen pound girl you know that is some crazy strength coming out of a girl. The hospital paperwork read that I was a 14-year-old female, bi-polar, and severely emotionally disturbed with violent outbursts of rage. I was to be on high security watch. I have no memory of any of the police taking me away or the majority of what happened that night. I blacked it all out. In my mind it was like it had never happened. This was all told to me after the incident by other people, including my therapist who was called to the scene.

My psychologist was sent to my house on an emergency call after I had been carted off to the hospital in full body restraints. They even had to put a mask on my face because if people got close enough to me I would bite them or spit on them. The whole incident was like something out of a movie. My therapist spoke to my now distraught mother and took pictures of my room and outside our house so that she could conduct a study on me. In her 35 years of practice, she had never heard of or seen anything like this before. I had made "crazy" history.

I was in Northridge Psychiatric Hospital for a long time after that specific incident. Each time I was sent away I was gone for so long. It took a long while for me to recover after being on Prozac for only three days. I was switched from Prozac to Lithium, then Lithium to Depakote, then Depakote to Zoloft, and the list went on. The concept or idea of no medication at all, clearly wasn't in anyone's interest but my own. It wasn't an option in the doctors' minds, I was too sick. At the age of fourteen, 13 different doctors all from different hospitals had diagnosed me as having bi-polar disorder. All of them were as ignorant as the next; the actual doctors prescribing me the medication never even spent enough time with me in our sessions to know what my true problems were. Instead, they were always in a rush and just prescribed pill after pill.

I had to attend therapy and speak about my feelings and problems. If I did not talk about them—or tried to trick them into believing that I was better when I was not—they would not let me leave. Being on medication does not always make you well, so as long as you are on it when you don't actually need it, you are not well. I learned what they wanted to hear so that's what I eventually gave them. None of it was ever real, just the correct words and phrases to get me out of there. By the time I had left the hospital, I was back on the first two medications that I was originally put on years earlier. I wish someone, anyone, had stepped in and taken me off those medications. There is no doubt in my mind that psychiatrists can be negligent and abusive to their patients, and in many cases, they are just writing prescriptions to kids with one thing in mind—money from the pharmaceutical companies, or a quick easy fix for a child instead of really looking into why the kid is struggling or the real circumstances. I still do not know today if I really am bi-polar or not.

I was finally sent home, and life went on. I would have good days and bad days. I would get so sad for no reason at all. It drove me crazy. I would cry so hard for so long that I would end up being tired for days. I put myself into exhaustion. Then some days I had great days and was happy and things were well. But I always felt in my mind that if something good happened, something bad was soon to follow because I believed that was how life worked.

One day I woke up at my dad's house, and I felt extremely depressed again. I couldn't figure out why. I had no real reason to be depressed; life was fine, and nothing bad was happening to me. Misty was even being nice for a change. She had braided my hair the day before and had even let me sit in the front seat of her car for the first time. I wondered if she felt sorry for me because I was constantly in and out of hospitals. I wonder if she felt guilty and thought it was her fault? I knew that she understood what being there was like, so maybe she had decided to change and would stop abusing me. Despite things being ok for a change, I felt really bad about myself. I obsessed about all the terrible things I had done and what a bad kid I was for such a long time. Why couldn't I just be happy? It felt like the sad feelings were never going to go away. They lasted so long.

I wanted to be happy, but I barely recalled what that emotion was supposed to feel like. Then I remembered a girl I had met in the hospital told me that cutting her wrists made her feel better. Ever since I had heard her say that, I had fantasized about doing it myself to rid myself of the emotional pain. Something had to take it away, right? I left the house and went in search of a box of razors from my dad's garage. I snuck one into my pocket and ran inside to my bathroom and locked the door. I hid the razor in the drawer and left it there. That night when everyone else was asleep, I took out the blade. I knew that everything that I was about to do was wrong but I couldn't help but want to do it anyway. I was sure that it would make me feel better. One part of me wanted to do it, while the other said don't do it. I didn't even know how to do it. I was so scared to cut myself for the first time, but I finally grew the courage to make the first cut. I did it. I took the razor blade and sliced into inside of my wrist. The feeling was much different than when Misty had cut me. I had control, and the guided pain felt good, like I was translating emotional pain into physical pain.

I kept on cutting myself and it was liberating. The pain inside was finally coming out. It made me feel a little better even if it would only last a short while. The horrible depression and pain that had stuck with me for so long suddenly vanished for a few moments. Each time I dug that blade into my skin and watched my blood spill out I couldn't think of anything else and that was a good feeling.

Most people think that someone cutting themselves is for attention or an attempted suicide. For me, it was neither that night. I was focused on me and trying to rid myself of pain. Young, confused, and on medication I'm sure had a lot do with my thinking and mindset at the time as well.

Soon after, my evening dose of Seroquel must have kicked in as I was done cutting myself because I recklessly unlocked my bathroom door, walked down the hall to my little sister's bedroom covered in blood, and stood in the dark with my arms dripping blood at my sides. I stood there for a while and then turned on the light to wake her up. "What are you doing?" she asked me. I held my arms up to her and said, "This is because of you; this is all your fault." I knew what I was doing was wrong but I couldn't stop myself from doing it. Her eyes grew big and she just sat there quiet and in shock—she was so scared. I have no idea why I went into her room or why I said that to her. It made no sense to me or to her. Nothing was her fault. I had just traumatized my baby sister and I knew what I was doing this time but it was as if my body was working but my brain was controlling me to do things I knew I shouldn't have been doing.

Something inside me snapped, and I ran back to my bathroom and sat on the floor and started crying hysterically. What had I just done? I hit myself in the head over and over again. I felt so stupid. I felt really bad about what I had just done to my sister. I was just adding to my list of f*ck ups and feeling like the sh*tiest person on the planet. I just sat there rocking back and forth on the floor of my bathroom crying until I was carried away in restraints and loaded into the back of another ambulance. I was heading back once again to another hospital.

Each time I went back to a hospital, I died a little more inside each time. My youth and my spirit were being stripped away. I was no longer a child; I was a psych patient now— even when I was home. Everyone treated me like I was crazy with serious problems but they hadn't seen anything yet.

Some things I learned:

- People look at cutters as either attention seekers or crazy people that have serious issues and look down upon them. You guys, these are the people we need to be lifting up. They are in so much pain emotionally and maybe they are seeking attention, so give it to them; they need it. Be the person that helps someone so desperately in need. You do not need to be a doctor but a good listener. That can really help someone. If I had someone I could talk to other than a doctor, maybe I would not have done that to myself.

- Cutting is not a real emotional release. Your brain is tricked into believing that from the adrenaline that surges when you self-inflict pain. Then a dopamine rise makes you feel good—and these complex physical reactions get mistaken for relief. There are better ways of dealing with that pain, and trust me; you do not want scars on your arms for the rest of your life. I have them, and they are embarrassing now. They do not go away.

- Most people that cut are driven to it. They do not have the tools to express how they feel (because they are medicated or feel helpless), so they hurt themselves instead. This compulsion is born from low self-esteem and severe emotional trauma. Do not blame someone for cutting, instead, try to be a friend to those people as they need friends more than anyone and help make sure they seek professional help, they need it.

Chapter 6

HIGH-School &
Prostitution

*"Forget what hurt you in the past, but
never forget what it taught you."*
SHANNON L. ALDER

was released from the hospital before entering high school and was getting ready to start ninth grade. Before even setting foot into high school I thought I was a lost cause, and I don't blame any of my family or friends for thinking that way about me. I attended Granada Hills High School. New school, new people, and the same scenario as always it felt like. I didn't know anyone who was going to be going there. I had given up on trying to be "normal" or "good" and instead decided I wasn't going to follow any rules and I was going to have shitty attitude because I really didn't care. I felt like nobody was going to respect me, so why should I respect them? Besides, everyone thought I was crazy...because I was.

A month into Granada Hills High and I was already skipping school and flunking all my classes. I didn't care about anyone or anything... including myself. I started getting into drugs. Not my prescriptions drugs, but illegal street drugs like acid and ecstasy. The first time I tried drugs I was hooked. I immediately loved them. They made me feel good. All this time of feeling bad and depressed and on my regular meds making me feel so terrible, these new drugs made me happy. How come the doctors weren't passing these drugs out, these actually helped me I thought to myself. I had finally found something in life I really liked. Drugs. You know how all parents warn their kids about hanging around the wrong people? The one kid that is a bad influence on everyone else? That was me, I was the wrong person to be around. Parents did not want their kids hanging out with me.

My freshman year was also the year I became sexually active. I got a boyfriend named Miller, and I lost my virginity to him. You know how that goes—I believed it was love, and thought I was in love with him. Every year my dad would take our family to a lake called Buena Vista to go camping and have fun waterskiing, jet skiing, and knee boarding. That year I invited Miller to come with us. My dad was called back into work and Misty was also working (the lake wasn't too far from where we lived), so it ended up being one of my friends, Miller, and his friend alone at the lake. My father always kept alcohol in his motorhome for entertaining friends and parties, so of course once he had left we snuck into the motorhome and raided the cabinets. There were gallons of hard liquor and we all got really drunk that day. I have to admit it was a pretty fun day. While the parents are away the teenagers will play. That night, in our tent—I had sex for the first time…on an air mattress…with one of my friends sleeping next to us on the same mattress. It wasn't romantic at all, special, or my ideal first time experience but nothing else was ideal in my life so I didn't really care. From that night on, I loved sex and wanted to do it all the time. Our relationship didn't last long after that. We eventually broke up because we went to different schools, and it was hard to see each other so we ended it. I was now doing drugs and having sex with a lot of different guys, mostly guys older than me, but I was far from grown up. In fact, because of doing drugs, having sex all the time, and the influence that drugs have on you, I began a new path that I really didn't expect or see coming.

One day when I was walking home from skipping school, a limo driver pulled off to the side of the road and stopped his limo next to me. He rolled down his window and asked me if I wanted a ride home. It was a nice limo, and I had never been in one before, so I got in. The driver asked me where I lived, so I gave him my address and we headed in the direction of my house. He was asking me all these questions and then out of nowhere he asked me if I wanted to make some money.

"Sure," I said, excited that I would be able to afford more drugs. It was becoming increasingly difficult to steal money from my parents. The limo driver pulled into a grocery store parking lot near my house and parked there. He got out and joined me in the back of the limo. Then he locked the doors and told me that if I gave him a blowjob, he would give me $100.00. I was shocked at the proposition and didn't expect it at all. I thought he was going to ask me if I wanted to wash his limo or something. He was a lot older than I was and he was overweight and sweaty. I was really disgusted by him but I wanted more drugs and with $100.00 I could buy a lot more drugs than I was used to buying. I asked him if anyone could see us inside the limo and he said no. The windows were tinted. He unzipped his pants and pulled his pants and underwear down to his knees. Then he put his hand behind my head and pushed it down onto his already erect penis. I was hesitant at first, but just thought about how good I would feel when I had those drugs in my hands. I started giving him a blowjob and he fondled my newly developing breasts and said things like, "Oh yeah!" and "You like sucking older men's cocks?" I couldn't wait for it to be over. Fortunately he came really fast so it went by quickly. When he was done, he handed me $100.00 in twenties. He had baby wipes conveniently located in the back seat, like he did this kind of thing all the time. He wiped himself off and gave me a baby wipe to wipe my mouth off and then he jumped back into the driver's seat and drove me home. It all happened so fast. I felt really dirty but I had also made $100.00 in less than a minute so I was excited about that. So I had my first escort experience at the young age of 14. This went on for a few months. One day I invited my friends after school to come home in the limo with me to get a ride home. I ended up having sex in the back of the limo with the old guy in front of all four of them.

Some of my friends thought it was cool that I had made $300.00 for having sex with him, but one of my friends was crying when we got out of the car and was really upset by all of it. I didn't care what she was thinking or that she was upset, all I cared about was making money and doing drugs. Drugs will have that affect on you; once you're addicted you will find a way to get them even if that means doing things you would never normally do.

I began attending a church youth group with a bunch of teenagers that met for Bible study. I wasn't into it, but my parents made me to go in an attempt to keep me out of trouble. I met a boy named Jason there and thought he was so cute! I was going to make him my boyfriend. I was obsessed with him. We ended up dating and hooking up, even though he went to another high school and was two grades above me. I thought I was the coolest girl in the world because I was dating a high school junior. I was one of the only freshman girls at my school that was dating a junior, which made me feel pretty awesome. I was still getting in trouble at school and I was such a bad kid, so naturally I hung out with other bad kids and decided to start my own girl gang. Yes, I know it sounds ridiculous, a little blonde white girl starting her own gang? Well before you get ahead of yourself let me just say we were some pretty bad ass white girls and if you ask anyone at our school they were scared of us and knew just how crazy we were. We, well I especially, wasn't scared of getting in trouble, dying, or anything for that matter. Those are types of people you should be scared of, as they think they have nothing to lose. Our little girl gang was called AS2. It stood for 'Ain't Scared of Sh★t' and it consisted of around 7-12 girls. We keyed cop cars, would graffiti school property, stole makeup from stores, ditched school, stole Slurpee's from 7-11, smoked cigarettes, did drugs, and partied hard. We were ridiculous to say the least. We were bored and troubled teenagers and really enjoyed causing trouble. It kept us entertained.

I remember one night we all went over to our friend Julie's house, her parents were super cool and let us throw parties there all the time. We would all sneak out of our houses at night and steal money from our parents to pitch in to have Julie's dad buy us a keg, vodka and whatever drugs we could get our hands on. This particular party I happen to get really wasted at. I remember a couple of us climbed onto the roof and took ecstasy pills and mixed it with acid. Let's just say some really weird shit happened that night. We were talking to aliens and riding on UFO's it was pretty awesome to say the least, until my mom came into to the party with one of her friends looking for me. That was one of my most embarrassing moments for me in high school. My mom found me at the party and dragged me out of there making a big scene in front of everyone there, what a buzz kill. I was so mad at her. She told me I was never allowed to go back over there again. But of course that didn't stop me. I kept going to Julie's parties until one night some guy I had never seen before pushed me into the bathroom and tried to rape me. I never went back there again after that night.

One day a new girl came to our school, Jill. She was very pretty, had blonde hair and blue eyes, and wanted to hang out with us. Our group or 'gang' was popular at school; especially for only being ninth graders and everyone knew us as the troublemakers and partiers. They knew we all did drugs and did whatever we wanted. No one in our group liked the new girl Jill. They said she was a fake bitch, but I gave her a chance and let her in our 'gang' because I knew what it was like being at a new school with no friends.

We became best friends and did everything together—until the day I found out that she had hooked up with my boyfriend behind my back. I was hurt, angry, and really unpredictable because I was mixing street drugs and my psychiatric medication. I was the last person Jill wanted to betray. I didn't care about getting in trouble for anything and I certainly didn't care about Jill anymore. I was going to make her pay for what she had done. I was infuriated with her.

I got one of my other friends in AS2 to steal my mom's car with me in the middle of the night. I was going to burn down Jill's house with her whole family inside it. No one has sex with my boyfriend and gets away with it, especially not my "best" friend. The fact that this happened brought up a lot of bad memories from childhood, my dad and my mom and the cheating, and the hurt that it caused my family. It just added to my hatred and anger.

There was a slight problem with my plan because I was only 14 years old and didn't even know how to drive but I somehow managed to drive my mom's car in the middle of the night to my friend's house who was going to help me. While I was backing out of my moms parking spot where we lived I accidentally ran into a cement divider as I was trying to figure out how the car worked. I really didn't care that I messed up my mom's car. I was on a mission. I picked up my friend and we headed to the store to buy gasoline. They didn't sell any at the drug store, so we stole some spray paint and a lot of nail polish remover instead. It was the most flammable stuff we could find or knew of at the time. We weren't the brightest of the bunch I will say that. When we arrived to Jill's house, I spray painted SLUT and WHORE all over her garage and the front of her house. Then we doused the front bushes with nail polish remover and lit a match. Once it lit, we ran back to the car as fast as we could so we wouldn't get caught. I never did see the damage from lighting Jill's house on fire because we weren't going to stick around to get caught. The damage must have been pretty bad though, because there were a ton of police officers at our school the next day. I was called to the principal's office and questioned on where I was the night before. I denied the whole incident and they had no evidence or proof against me, so they let me go. Jill's home wasn't enough for me though; regardless of how much or how little damage had been done to her house. I hadn't personally confronted her yet. During lunchtime, I planned for my friends to lure Jill to the bathroom. My plan was to get her in the bathroom, cut her hair off really short with a pair of scissors and beat her over the head with a wrench for having sex with my boyfriend. I wanted to teach that shifty bitch a lesson. As planned, my friends got Jill into the bathroom but she must have had an idea that I knew what she had done because she was terrified to see me in the bathroom. As soon as Jill entered, a friend of mine locked the bathroom door so that no one else could come in. I didn't say a word to Jill, I just punched her as hard as I could in her pretty little face. She fell down to the ground and I drug her by her hair into one of the bathroom stalls. I hit her over the head with the wrench and then I pulled out my scissors from my hoodie and started chopping off chunks of her blonde hair. I cut about half of her hair off before I shoved her head into the toilet and tried to drown her. One of my friends saw that I was taking it too far and pulled me off her and she ran out of the bathroom crying.

Later that day, while sitting in my English class, some police officers entered the room. They asked if there was a Channon Rose in the class. I raised my hand and said, "Yup, that's me." I knew why they were there and I didn't care. They handcuffed me in front of my whole class and said that I was under arrest for arson, battery, and attempted murder. They read me my rights and took me to juvenile hall. I sat in handcuffs and ankle cuffs in a holding cell for a few hours. Then I was put into juvenile hall. They called my mother and once they found out that I was bi-polar and had been hospitalized in the past, they released me to the mental institution instead of staying in juvenile hall. In addition to going back to another mental hospital, I was now kicked out of the entire Los Angeles School District for what I had done. I was then placed in Special Education for being emotionally disturbed.

Here is what I learned:

- **Don't do DRUGS! They might give you temporary happiness but in the long run they do so much damage to your life, it is not worth it. Just watch the show Intervention. That show should change your mind about wanting to do drugs.**
- When you're young, the things that you care the most about are usually things that won't matter to you at all when you get older like friendship battles, young relationships, peer pressure, etc. When people cheat, there are always two or more people involved. One person isn't always 100% to blame. Many people are immature, not happy, not satisfied, or it could be any number of things. It usually stems from insecurity. Do not do what I did; it's not worth it, I promise. It gives the other person a sense of control and power over

you. Don't give them the satisfaction of knowing that their negative action will hurt you. If they go behind your back and do something to hurt you, they aren't good enough to be in your life anyway. You are better than that. Having that on my record for life for some girl who is a complete stranger to me now is not worth it. Thankfully, I was able to have those records expunged, because I was a minor but that is not always possible. Do not hurt people. I did all that over what? A boy! A cheating scumbag boy! Who is a total loser now. Totally not worth my time. PLEASE LEARN FROM MY MISTAKES. I promise you it isn't worth it.

- Do not get into strangers' cars—I could have been easily raped and killed, and although what that limo driver did was sick and twisted, I made the choice to get in the car, so it was just as much my fault. Think hard about things before you do them. Once you do something you shouldn't have done you can't go back in time and take it back. If you think that what you are about to do is wrong, don't do it because it most likely is wrong.

- Crime really does not pay. People that live in that life hurt themselves over and over again. Every bad decision comes back to haunt you—so choose not to make them. You do not have to be good, but choose to not hurt yourself either. Years later, you have to deal with the emotional repercussions of your actions and it's not an easy thing do. Remember, negative actions bring forth more negativity into your life and at some point we all need to pay for our wrongdoings. Choose to be a good person not a bad one, you will feel so much better when you know you are doing good in the world. Remember karma is only a bitch, if you are.

Chapter 7

School for Disturbed Youth

*"Sometimes people with the worst pasts
create the best futures."*

ANONYMOUS

What happens to bad kids when they get kicked out of normal schools? Well they put them where the rest of the bad kids go, a "special" school. I was sent to a "special" school for kids that had been kicked out of public school or could not function well in normal schools. "Special" was code for "where the bad kids go," and we all knew it. It is called Special Ed, but it is the Special Ed for kids who are bad and can't get through school without special help. They put all of us in one convenient location.

There were so many desperate, unruly, criminal, violent, and lost kids in that place. The school was called North Hills Prep. Many of the kids were more messed up than I was, if you can believe that. There were heroin addicts, meth heads, potheads, psychopaths and anything else you could possibly imagine. If a kid was REALLY bad, they were sent there. The classes at that school were a joke. The teachers barely taught us anything and schoolwork was rarely assigned because no one would do it anyway. Each class had about six students, and some of the kids even smoked meth in the back of class, to give you an idea of the learning environment and the entire situation there.

The teachers knew about most of the stuff that took place, but I had a sense that the teachers felt like many of the kids were beyond saving. I'm sure a lot of the kids' parents felt the same way, which is why we were there, and why there are schools like that in the first place. There was even a section on campus where kids could smoke cigarettes, which was new to me. I hadn't seen that before. We called it "the cage" because it was all fenced in and secure. Between every school period, I smoked cigarettes there even though none of us were of age to be smoking in the first place, but it was nice and convenient for us smokers. By the beginning of tenth grade I was smoking a pack a day. There weren't very many kids at that school, so friend choices were very limited. Not only that, but as you might guess the kids there most likely wouldn't have been the best influences anyways in terms of good friends.

I eventually became friends with Celine and Kay. They were both addicted to meth. They were really nice to me though and I didn't really have anybody else at that school to hang with or talk to. They asked me if I wanted to hang out with them after school, so I agreed since I didn't have any friends at that school yet. They introduced me to smoking meth, which up until that point I was too afraid to try. I really didn't want to do it, but I was peer pressured into trying it. Normally, I would peer pressure other people to do things, so this was a first being pushed into doing anything. I took my first hit and my whole world changed. I was hooked. I had never felt so high in my life! I felt so happy, a feeling that I had missed and longed for. I always wanted to feel that way, feel happy and not feel sad anymore. In an instant, and because of the immediate gratification, I was addicted to crystal meth and the feeling it gave me.

I smoked meth whenever I could get my hands on it. I stole from my parents and started escorting again to make more money to buy more drugs. I was in high school and had a handful of clients that I escorted for.

Soon, my drug problem got really bad. Meth is a drug that can ruin your life really fast. It's cheap, the high lasts a long time, it makes you skinny because you lose your appetite, and it's extremely addicting. Among other negative effects that occurred from smoking meth, one obvious thing that happened is I had lost a lot of weight. My dad and Misty were completely oblivious to anything that was going on. My mom on the other hand was beginning to suspect that something was wrong with me though. She questioned me and asked if I stopped eating and at first I think she thought my eating disorder was back but then she suspected I was on drugs and of course a drug addict's response is always NO. I said she was crazy and lied about everything. She was suspicious and rightfully so. You act weird and do strange things when you're on drugs.

My mom didn't trust anything I was telling her anymore so one day she went through my things and found a pack of cigarettes in my backpack. She completely flipped out on me, broke all my cigarettes in front of me and flushed them down the toilet. It wasn't always easy to get cigarettes being underage. I had to wait outside liquor stores and pay random strangers to buy me cigarettes. That night my mom brought a pack of cigarettes home and forced me to smoke the whole pack until I got sick. Her mother had died of lung cancer from smoking, so she was very disappointed in me and lectured me on smoking and how it killed her mother. Making me smoke all those cigarettes and getting sick didn't make me want to quit smoking, it just made me angry, want to rebel, and do drugs even more.

I didn't like being told what to do and I hated authority figures. I had lost my trust in authority figures many years ago as a young girl from all the sh*t I had already been put through. I despised them, my mom, and anyone else who wanted to tell me what to do. If they wanted me to do something, I was going to do the opposite just to piss them off. Adults were never around when I needed them, and they didn't prevent bad things from happening to me in the past so I didn't care about what they thought anymore. I had lost all respect for them.

I wasn't happy at home for so many reasons and because of it, I ran away from home multiple times during my childhood because I wanted to escape my life and my circumstances. I was beyond depressed and desperately unhappy when I was at home. I would run away from home and do drugs to feel better. Most of the people I hung out with at this point were older than me. It was a way to escape my life, which I hated. In reality, I hated myself most of all and the drugs made me feel better about myself.

So I kept doing drugs, and it didn't matter what drugs they were as long as I could escape my reality for awhile, I was going to do them. There was a carnival that a couple friends from school were going to that night and I had asked my dad to drop me off and pick me up a few hours later. While we were walking around the carnival there were these hippies walking around asking people if they wanted to buy shrooms. I bought some but I had never done mushrooms before. They sold us each a bag and I ate the whole bag. I thought it would be fun to be high on shrooms at the carnival. I didn't realize that you are only supposed to eat one mushroom. I ate the whole freaking bag! I started tripping balls to the wall. At first it was really fun, I was hallucinating and all the colors were so much brighter, and the sounds and smells of everything were much more intense. I must have met some guys that night because I ended up going home with them. I was so high and was really out of it I had no idea what was going on. Once I got to their house I started having a really bad trip. I took WAY too many shrooms and sh*t was not going well. I was starting to see really scary things like the devil talking to me, and cats were attacking me. Light bulbs were being shattered all around me and it felt like the world was going black and it was the end of the world. Then I felt like I was in hell, it was the worst experience I have ever had on drugs. I was freaking out. Then as I was having this horrible trip this guy that took me home started trying to have sex with me. I kept telling him to stop that I was freaking out but he just kept telling me I was fine. It was awful. The whole night I felt like the bad trip was never going to go away. I ended up passing out at this stranger's house that night and waking up naked having no idea where I was. I was scared and wanted to go home. I felt violated and my dad was probably wondering where I was because he was supposed to pick me up that night at the carnival. We didn't have cell phones back then so he had no way of reaching me. I asked the guy to take me home and I didn't even know what his name was. When I got home I walked through the door and my dad just looked at me with a, 'I am pissed at you face and you are in trouble' but he never really did anything to punish me. I don't know if he just didn't care, figured I was a lost cause or if he was just glad I was alive. I told myself after that night I was going to stick to doing meth. I never did shrooms again after that night. I had a similar experience with acid and never did acid again after that either.

Between the drugs I was doing and the medication the psychiatrists had put me on I was a disaster and should have died many times. I overdosed on Vicodin, and then a few months later overdosed on meth. I was like a cat with nine lives. The meth made me skinny, but I was too skinny, I looked sick to everyone else but I liked the way I looked. I felt sexy when I was high. I would run away from home for 3 days getting high, and when I would eventually get back home I would sleep for days. I skipped school all the time, and I wanted to sleep my life away when I wasn't high. Coming down off drugs sucks, and you feel like sh*t. Not to mention, when you're up for several days on drugs, your body eventually crashes and you sleep for almost the same amount of time. It's hard on your system.

I was basically doing whatever I wanted whenever I wanted and none of it was good. I can't imagine how my parents dealt with it. It was just a bad situation all the way around, for them, and for me. If they would try and talk to me, I wouldn't listen or care, and if my parents did nothing at all, then what? I would just get worse because I would think they didn't care. It was a lose lose situation either way. It became apparent to my mom that something had to change. None of us could keep going the way that things were headed so my mom decided to take action. One night she came into my room in the middle of the night to give me my prescribed medicine, which wasn't out of the ordinary for her to do. At least I thought it was my prescribed medicine. I swallowed the pill and told her to leave me alone because I needed to sleep. A few hours later, I woke up surrounded by people. My mom, my dad, and my mom's friend Sue were all in my room. I felt really weird and drugged, but not high like the drugs I would usually do. I was completely out of it. The whole situation was odd, and I did not know what was going on. Then my mom said, "Chan you're going away for awhile."

I tried to move, but I couldn't. I was very confused. The three of them pulled me out of bed and started to put clothes on me. "Why can't I move?" I muttered. My mother told me I felt weird because of

96

the pill she gave me. She repeated that I was going away for a while. I had heard her the first time, but I didn't understand. Where were they taking me? They didn't want to tell me where they were taking me. I started to get scared but whatever my mom had given me made me so weak and tired I didn't have the energy to keep asking what they were doing with me. I figured they were sending me back to the hospital, but I wasn't that lucky. I was going somewhere much worse. My mom had drugged me so that they could put me on a plane and send me to a lockdown facility for all girls in another state. She was sending me away, shipping me off for the state to care for me. She knew if she had told me, I would have just run away. I was so out of it that my dad had to carry me to the car so they could take me to the airport. My dad drove with my mom and her friend to take me to the airport which was odd because my mom and dad didn't normally do things together so I knew something bad was about to happen to me, I just wasn't sure what. When we got to the airport my dad gave me a hug, which was also out of the ordinary. He never hugged me. That was the last time I was going to see my dad for a long time and I hadn't a clue. The airport provided my parents with a wheelchair to get me safely onto the plane. My mom had all of this planned out for weeks. I remember I woke up a few times on the airplane, but only for a few moments, and then would fall back asleep. That one little pill definitely did its job of knocking me out. As a matter of fact, the doctors had told my mom to give me only half of the pill, but she gave me the whole thing instead because she was scared I would wake up and try to run away. I was completely out of it for three entire days. I don't have any recollection of my mom flying with me or even dropping me off at the facility.

When I finally woke up, I was in a small, cold, dark room that was really stuffy and smelled like feet. I don't remember getting off the plane, the ride to wherever the hell I was going, or arriving at this dump of a room. There was an African American girl next to me. I had absolutely no idea where I was. I guess the pill I was given makes you forget things that happened. It causes temporary amnesia.

I asked the girl in the twin bed next to me where I was. She sucked her teeth and in the most ghetto voice I had ever heard, said, "Gurrrrrl, you're in Excelsior Youth Center in Colorado." I began to freak out, I kept looking around the room, hoping it was a bad acid trip or something, but it wasn't. It was real. I was in a lock down facility for all girls in a completely different state and far away from home. Stuck in another new place, confused, scared, and angry. I felt so betrayed yet again but this time by my own mother. How could she do this to me I thought to myself? How can you just ship away your little girl when I needed my mother the most?

The girl in my room was Latoya. She was from Philly, and she was ghetto as f*ck. She was my roommate for the next several months. She was such a bitch to me because she thought I was some rich white girl. I was told that I would be spending my life locked away in that sh★thole of a facility, until I was better.

The "center" was a giant old house with 20 different rooms in it, but far from being a mansion, it closely resembled a small, compact prison. I lived there with 40 other girls in one house, locked away from the rest of the world. Every window had bars on it, and we had guards and staff 24 hours throughout the house. We weren't allowed to use phones and we were only allowed to call home once a week for 10 minutes. Family members weren't even allowed to visit. This place was worse than jail!

It was a facility for girls run by the state. Girls were to work a program and go to school until they were better and could leave. Some girls had been there for 5 years! I knew there was no way I was going to be there for five years and knew I would do whatever I needed to be able to get out of there in the least amount of time possible. When I initially arrived at the lockdown facility, my therapist that I was assigned to took me off all my medications. I went into withdrawal from all the street drugs I was on, and also withdrawals from my prescribed medications. Cigarettes weren't allowed either, so that was another withdrawal to deal with. I was so sick for the entire first month I was there. My body physically had to deal with so much all at one time. Emotionally, I was dealing with just as much. I felt sick that I was betrayed and that my parents had drugged me and shipped me off to this place. My parents had just handed me over to the state to deal with, not to mention in another state. The psych wards and hospitals I was used to were at least near my home, and I never spent too much time in those places, at least not longer than a month at a time. This place was no joke; I was very far away and for a very long time. I felt trapped. I had never felt so low. It took me months to adjust and get used to living in a place like that. I really just wanted to be good so I could get out of there. So that was what I really began to focus on and put my energy towards. I can say I did the very best I could. I finally started to feel normal and level headed again because I was finally off all the drugs. My head could start to function on it's own for the first time in what seemed like forever. Even before I was using illegal drugs, the doctors had me on so many psych meds that were wrong for me which distorted my thinking and behavior for years. Since I was free from all the meds, my assignments and classes were making more sense and I got straight A's. I was in an environment that knew I had issues and worked with me so I was doing well, and I worked the program and did everything everyone told me to do. For once, I actually obeyed the rules and paid attention and it was paying off.

It was not easy living with 40 different girls in one house and having to go to school with them. When you are with that many different girls you have a lot of different personalities and people fight. When you spend 24 hours a day with them, 7 days a week, it gets rough to say the least. I have to admit I absolutely HATED that place when I first got there, and for the first few months I still hated it. But I came to realize that even though I hated my parents for putting me there and felt betrayed by them, it was probably one of the best places they could have put me. Excelsior saved my life. It is not a pleasant place to be but it was the right place for me to be at that time in my life. I probably would have ended up dead in a ditch somewhere if my mother hadn't sent me there. I just didn't feel that way most of the time I was there. I was doing much better though. I worked really hard. I made some friends while I was there that I am still friends with today.

Let me give you an idea of what it was like being in EYC. There were a bunch of cottages that girls were assigned to. I was in a cottage that was off campus. It was called Columbine; it was the only cottage at the time that was off campus. We had two vans that would drive us to school each day, the rock van and the rap van. I would alternate between the two each day when we went to school. It was kind of fun driving to school because we got to listen to music and all the girls would sing along with the radio on the way to school.

At school we were with all the girls from all the different cottages on campus. The girls were from either broken homes or had traumas in their lives as well. They were drug addicts, suicidal, had anger management problems and the list goes on. There was one girl I always saw at school that had cutting scars all over her face and body. The cuts were made so deep that she had keloid scars so they were raised really bad and very noticeable. I always felt so bad for her. There was another girl who always pulled her hair and eyelashes out and that always gave me the willies. A lot of other girls had mental illnesses. It was a rough place but we all had one thing in common, we all needed serious help.

I wrote a lot of letters home because that was really the only way to communicate with my family. My mom saved one of my letters that I sent to her so I am going to share what I wrote in response to a letter she wrote me:

Mom,

Trust me I miss you WAY more. I love getting your letters, even though I only get one every 2 weeks. That is funny how you and dad tease over who gets my letters and when. Yeah, I write you a lot because it is the only way I can talk to you other than my once a week ten minute phone call. I am glad you are proud of me because I am trying my hardest to get myself together here. I am glad I got a chance at a new beginning too because I needed one bad. I know it has taken you along time to try and help me but it was worth it all because now I am in a perfect place and it is helping me. It is study time right now and I have some free time so you asked me to explain where things got out of hand. I guess I was being left home alone a lot of the time and I didn't have anything to do, but I think most of it came from not getting any attention from you and dad. I felt like you didn't care about me as much or didn't want to spend time with me. I needed love and attention from you and when I never got it I felt really unloved. I felt like being rebellious always got me attention even though it was negative attention I was happy I got something. I couldn't get attention by getting good grades because Birdy already did that so I felt like it was the only way. But I have changed, I am working on how to get your attention without being bad all the time. The other part of it was being put into North Hills Prep, that school is a death trap, even the kids that go there say that. You either need to do meth or sell it to be cool. When I got high all my hurting on the inside went away. I don't expect you to understand it but just know I am getting better. Guess what mom! I got to level 2! We have certain jobs around the house, kind of like chores and we have to keep everything really clean. I think I will clean more when I get home because I don't want to get in trouble and I want to make you happy. Oh my god mom, you aren't going to believe this but I got athletes feet! It is SO gross! I have even been showering with sandals on and walking around the house with slippers on, this house has fungus and it is NASTY, I went to the school nurse but she said she can't help me, can you send me spray stuff for my feet please, and chips! I miss chips the food here isn't that great and I just really want to come home. I miss you a lot. I am never going to be bad again, I promise mom. I am sad I am missing the family reunion and Christmas, and Halloween and every holiday. Mom I love you. Write me back please I really need to hear from you, it keeps me focused and gives me motivation while I am here.

Love Channon xoox

That was just one of hundreds of letters I sent while I was living at EYC.

A lot of things were new to me during my stay at Excelsior, one of which was living with a new girl every few months. We changed roommates frequently, I guess to encourage social interaction or something. I don't really know why to be honest. I had one roommate named Aura, she was a very interesting person. She was also from California. She was pretty crazy though and she always kept me entertained. We had goldfish in our cottage and one day she took one out of the tank and ate it. I was like holy sh*t you just ate that fish, GROSS! Aura ate a lot of weird sh*t. She ate gluesticks, crayons, paper, and anything else that you aren't supposed to eat, she ate it. She was very creative and I liked that about her, she made cool art and was always nice to me. One day Aura had been acting weird, I mean she was a total weirdo but she was acting weirder than usual. She was really quiet which was unlike her and kept to herself most of the day. I just figured she was having a bad day so I let her be. Then I was woken up in the middle of the night by one of the staff that had worked there. She asked me to go upstairs with her because she needed to ask me some questions. When I walked into the office they made me aware that Aura had been sent in an ambulance to the emergency room because she drank a bottle of Windex. She tried to kill herself with a bottle of Windex! I was shocked, I had no idea, she was my roommate and I didn't even know she wasn't in her bed when they asked me to go upstairs. I never even heard her leave our room that night. They asked me a bunch of questions and I just told them I had no idea about anything and that all I noticed is that she was acting strange that day. They sent me back to my room but I obviously couldn't sleep, I was worried about Aura. A few days later Aura was sent back to our cottage and she seemed like she was back to her normal self. I was upset that she didn't talk to me or even let me know she was upset, but she was acting normal again and back to eating weird stuff. After that incident all of our household supplies we used for chores had to be locked up and checked out and checked back in as soon as we were done using them.

I had another experience I will never forget with a different roommate who was severely depressed all the time. I ended up becoming close with her and we would write music together on her guitar and come up with fun songs. One morning I had opened my closet to get ready for school and I found her hanging in it. She was dead when I found her. She had hung herself in the middle of the night with one of her belts. I was pretty traumatized by that. I screamed when I found her and immediately dropped to the ground. I covered my face and my eyes and I couldn't believe it. I didn't want to look at her and I didn't want it to be real. I was so sad and mad that I couldn't have helped her. I kept crying and I felt like it was my fault because I was her roommate. I thought maybe I should have talked to her or maybe there was something I could have done to have changed her mind. It was too late though. She was gone. Our cottage had held a debriefing to help us mourn our loss. It was one of the most awful things I had ever seen. It took months for me to get over the initial shock. It is still something I haven't gotten over and probably never will.

Towards the end of my stay there was another time I was bunked with this girl named Cami. She was kind of boyish like a tomboy, and I was pretty sure she was a lesbian. She came on to me one day and we started kissing and touching each other and one thing led to another and we ended up having sex. Girl sex, lesbian sex, whatever you want to call it, it was pretty hot and exciting until we got caught. We got in a lot of trouble for inappropriate behavior and it set me back quite a bit for getting out of the facility early so I never did it again. For awhile I thought I liked girls and thought I was a lesbian until later when I got out and remembered boys existed in the world. It might be hard to explain but being in a facility with all girls for a year with nobody else around, the only intimacy you have is other girls. The incident with my roommate set me back a little but I stayed focused and worked my ass off to get out of there as soon as I could.

During my stay I got a phone call from my mother telling me that Misty had my dad arrested and put in jail. I couldn't believe it, I got so angry. My mother and father were going to try to sort things out between them and try and get back together, but Misty found out. She told my dad that if she couldn't have him, no one could. Misty had her own daughter lie and say that my dad had sexually molested her. She went to every extent possible to make everyone believe her lies. She went to the newspaper, all the sports teams my dad coached, and anyone else that she could try and influence her story upon. It was a huge messy ordeal and my dad sat in jail until his trial. Misty is very lucky that I was locked away at the time because I would have killed her myself. Hatred is not a strong enough word for my feelings about that woman. All these accusations about my dad emotionally destroyed him. He was in jail, stressed, and his reputation was ruined and everyone thought my dad was a child molester! Thankfully, my dad was found not guilty and was released from jail but that wasn't until months later. Misty had now stole months from my dad's life and put him through hell just as she had done with me years earlier. When the trial was over and my dad was finally released, my mom and dad ended up moving back in together. Shortly after all that happened, my year was up in the Excelsior lockdown facility and because of my good behavior and good grades and I was released after my one-year stay. Thank God!

This is what I learned:

- At the time, I absolutely *hated* my mother for sending me to a lockdown facility for all girls in Colorado; in fact, I felt betrayed by her for years. But as I got older, I realized she was just trying to do the right thing for me. I thank her now because who knows where I would be if I was not sent there—maybe dead or in jail for life for killing Misty. Remember, things happen for a reason. We might not always know the reason why something is occurring. It might be good, it might be bad, but later in the future you will probably realize a benefit from it, or at least a very important learning experience.

- Sometimes our parents do things to us, or maybe don't let us do things for a good reason. When we are teenagers, we think we know a lot, but we really don't. We should listen to our parents. Most of the time they are right, and I wish I had listened to my mom more often growing up. I listen to everything she says now, and I am a grown woman.

- When one door closes, another one opens, and it often happens to be something way better than you would have thought, so stay positive in your thought process when something awful happens in your life.

★ *If someone you know ever commits suicide don't spend your life thinking it was your fault or that you could have saved them. I spent a lot of time feeling like there was something I should have done, but now I know it wasn't my fault. It was a very unfortunate experience and I hope no one ever has to go through that.*

Chapter 8

My Near Death Experience

*"It doesn't matter what life you were born into;
it is up to you whether or not you want to live
happy. You have that choice, so take it."*

Once I had arrived home from Excelsior Youth Center, my mom decided that since I had been doing so well, she would put me back in a private school again. She thought it would be good for me. So I was enrolled into Los Angeles Baptist at the beginning of my junior year. I was doing well back in a normal school. I enjoyed being back at a private school, I made new friends, and I was staying out of trouble until one day when I found out there was a party that all of my friends were going to. This kid's parents were out of town so he was throwing a party and coincidentally, my parents were also out of town. My mom and dad were away on a houseboat trip, so they would never even know I had gone to a party and I wouldn't be able to get in trouble. I got ready at my house and my friend Jess picked me up. She was a friend from school, and one of the few of our friends who had a car, so she drove a few of us to the party.

I ended up getting really drunk at the party. Clearly, that was not my intention but everyone else was drinking and I wanted to have fun too. I was locked up for so long I needed to have fun, and besides it wasn't like I was smoking meth or anything. I had lost my tolerance for alcohol though, I thought I could drink as much as I used to so I got pretty drunk fast. Nothing out of the ordinary really happened at the party, but I must have lost track of time, or not been paying attention because at the end of the night when the party was being broken up by the cops (us private school kids sure know how to party) I couldn't find Jess to take me home. I think she ended up leaving early but I didn't know. Maybe she told me she was leaving, but I don't remember her saying goodbye. I looked around for her for awhile, but she was nowhere to be found. So I lost my ride home and needed to find another one. I saw one of my math tutors from school at the party and assumed that since he was kind of a dorky kid he wouldn't be drunk and could drive me home safely. I asked him for a ride, and he agreed to take me home.

My math tutor was with one of his friends, so the three of us got into his old four-door Bronco and started driving. The guys asked if I wanted to go to the beach for a little bit before we went home, which was cool with me, I was still drunk so it sounded like fun. So we headed to the beach and hung out there for a few hours. The guys drank beer while we were there, but I was so drunk I really didn't think much about it or pay attention to how much they were actually drinking. We all started to get pretty tired and it was really late, or I should say it was really early morning at that point but it was still dark out. We decided to head home for the night. We got into the car and I jumped in the backseat behind the driver and put my seatbelt on. I was exhausted and just wanted to sleep so I ended up taking the top strap of the seatbelt and pulled it over my head and pushed it behind my back, but still leaving the waist belt on so I was able to lay down sideways on the backseat while still having my seatbelt on. Shortly thereafter I fell asleep.

When I woke up, I faintly looked around, and realized our car wasn't moving. We were stopped in the middle of the freeway. Completely dead stopped on the 405 Freeway in Los Angeles in the middle of the night. The glass was missing from all the windows in our car, everything was dead quiet, and it felt as if I were in a dream. A nightmare would have been a better description.

I barely managed to look up at the guy sitting in the passenger seat. He stared back at me with a blank terrified look on his face. He didn't say anything. He didn't have to. His face said it all. I immediately tried to get up and when I did, I must have quickly gone into shock. I have no memory from that moment on except for a really loud noise and people around me sounding like they were in a hurry. It was an emergency helicopter landing on the 405 Freeway. There had been a horrific accident on the freeway, and I was in the middle of it. The helicopter was there for me. One of the biggest, if not the biggest freeway in Los Angeles California was completely shut down for the emergency rescue helicopter to airlift me to a hospital.

On September 5th of 2001, the driver of our car, my math tutor, was drunk and fell asleep at the wheel while driving. We were traveling at 60mph when we hit a stopped MTA bus. Our car was completely demolished. The fire department had to cut the car open to get all three of us out. My injuries were so bad that I had to be airlifted to UCLA hospital because they did not think I was going to make it. I didn't know it when they loaded me onto the helicopter, but I had broken my back in three different places; I had shattered L1–L3 in my vertebrae and was paralyzed from the waist down. I had also lacerated my spleen and kidney and sustained severe internal bleeding. I urinated myself when I went into shock. I suffered life-threatening injuries and the odds of surviving the crash were not in my favor.

My math tutor broke his jaw on the steering wheel, had a lacerated spleen and kidney, and sustained severe internal injuries as well. The passenger had some internal bleeding, but he walked away from the crash. Both boys were taken in an ambulance to Northridge Hospital, and they both had to have emergency surgeries performed to stop their internal bleeding. The guy that was in the passenger seat told me months after the accident that when he looked back at me, I was screaming. I have no recollection at all of ever screaming. I think the trauma was too severe and your body and mind go into another place.

It's crazy how one stupid decision can change your entire life. When I finally arrived at the hospital, the medical staff needed to somehow reach my family and let them know I was there. It took the staff awhile to get my parents' correct phone numbers, but they finally reached my mother and told her I had been in an accident. She was furious because she thought that I had gotten into trouble again. She had no idea how hurt I was. When a hospital calls a family member or loved one, they always make it seem like the accident or incident was not that bad, because they don't want people rushing to the hospital and causing additional harm to themselves or others.

When my mom arrived at the hospital and saw me lying in the hospital bed hooked up to machines and in a neck brace, she passed out, and they had to put her in the bed next to me in the emergency room. When she came to, she called my dad and told him to get the rest of the family to the hospital because I was not in good shape.

My whole family came to see me, even my brother who I almost never saw. They thought I was going to die in the hospital that day, so they all wanted the chance to say goodbye to me. I was in a coma-like state and have no memory of them even being there. I would fade in and out, but I was on so much morphine I couldn't really comprehend my situation or understand the circumstances and the reality of what happened and what had happened to me. The doctors needed to do surgery on my back and another one on my stomach to try and stop the internal bleeding. They decided to wait and see if the internal bleeding would stop on its own because they couldn't perform both surgeries at the same time. My mom later told me that I looked 9 months pregnant when I was in the ICU because my stomach was so large from all the internal bleeding.

Eventually, after a few days in the ICU the bleeding started slowly subsiding on it's own, but I still needed major surgery done for my back injuries. The doctors scheduled my surgery for September 11, 2001. But then the unexplainable happened. Two hijacked planes were flown into the Twin Towers in New York City. If you remember that day, it was mass panic, sorrow, and an utterly disgusting act of terrorism against the United States on our soil. Our hospital operating rooms were immediately shut down, and everyone was on high alert in case something happened in Los Angeles, not to mention the entire United States. They wanted all of the operating rooms open in case there was another attack and they were needed.

The chief spinal surgeon at UCLA had to fight against staggering odds to get me into the operating room that day to perform my surgery. He fought for my life. He had already prolonged my surgery too long. He had to convince the hospital that I was just as bad, if not worse than anyone else who would be brought into the hospital that day. He was granted permission to operate on me on the 11th but only after a meeting with the directors of the hospital. Despite the commotion of the 911 attacks that morning, and everyone having to set aside personal feelings during that terrible day, the chief surgeon and his team started to perform a difficult surgery that would take hours. When the doctors cut my back open, they were surprised at what they found. It was much worse than they could have ever expected. Usually when you cut open a person's back for surgery, you have to cut through a lot of muscle to get to the vertebrae. However, in my case, I had no muscle to cut through; it had all been ripped apart during the impact of the crash.

The plan was to fuse together L1–L5 of my vertebrae to restore stability.

They also discovered a bone fragment that had been pushing on my spinal cord, which was most likely the cause of my paralysis. They removed it, and then they took bone from my hip and put it into my back—it was one of the worst injuries they had seen in a long time. The doctors were going to do everything they could, but my parents were devastated when they were told that I would never walk again, especially my dad. He had watched me play sports and coached me my whole life and it was the one thing I was really good at. I think we had all hoped that one day I would earn a sports scholarship to college and further my education despite my earlier behaviors.

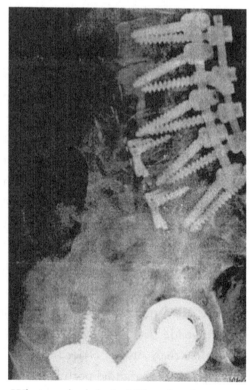

What my back looked like after the surgery

The surgery took twelve hours to complete, and when it was done, the doctors came out of the operating room with some surprising news. Even though the damage had been much more extensive than the doctors originally thought, a miracle had happened. I now had feeling in my lower extremities again. The doctor said, "I don't know what higher power you believe in, but whatever it is, it was with Channon today because she has feeling in her lower extremities again. It is a miracle, I have never seen anything like this before". The doctor did warn my parents that everything wasn't perfect though. I still had a lot of recovery and I might still have numbness in parts of my legs, but with enough physical therapy and rehab, I should be able to walk again in a few months.

I believe that my accident was a blessing in disguise as it reminded not only me, but also our entire family how precious life can be. My accident brought my parents closer together but it also brought my dad and brother back together after not talking to one another for a long time. (My brother stopped talking to my dad when Misty told him he had molested her daughter.) Knowing that my accident brought back a relationship between my brother and father meant so much to me. In fact, it brought our whole family closer

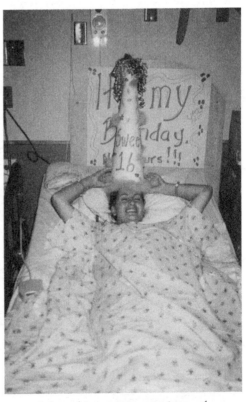

Me waking up on my sixteenth birthday in the hospital

together. On my sixteenth birthday (5 days after my back surgery) I was finally "waking up" and actually able to understand where I was, what had happened, and I was coherent.

I was confined to a hospital bed after my surgery for what seemed like forever and I was in a lot of physical pain. Probably the worst pain I've had in my life was trying to recover from that accident. But I was happy inside because I knew that one day I would be able to walk again. You may not think that I had to re-learn how to walk, but I did, and it was very upsetting because even though I knew how to walk, it felt as if I had never walked before and it took a ton of physical therapy to get me just to sit up in bed let alone be able to walk. That was a big struggle for me and was very upsetting to me day after day. Not only was it extremely hard but I was also in excruciating pain so it made it that much harder.

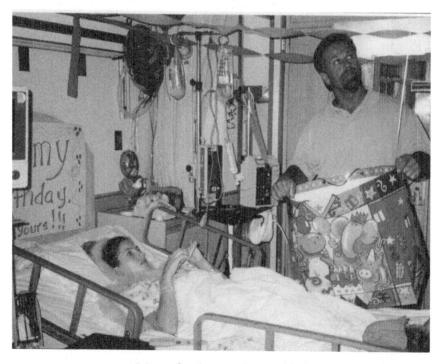

Me confined to my hospital bed

During my stay at the hospital, I shared a room with a girl who needed a heart transplant. We became good friends because we spent every waking hour together. I felt so sad for her; I wanted to help her so much that I wanted to give her my heart.

While I was in recovery, I had good days and I had bad days. I think that's fairly typical though. One day I was physically feeling pretty good and I wanted to go down to the gift shop in the hospital to get my roommate a gift. My mother asked one of the nurses if I could go down with her to the gift shop unsupervised (meaning without a nurse) because I was not allowed to leave my room without a nurse or a physical therapist. If I left my room, it was hospital policy to always have a staff member with me because of my extensive injuries in case something happened. The nurse never looked at my chart; she just told my mom it was fine and wouldn't be a problem if I was feeling up to it. My mom took me down in my wheelchair and I got my roommate a really cute stuffed animal and a bracelet so that she could hide her ugly hospital wristbands that we all had to wear.

Once we got back to my floor on the way back from the gift shop, I asked my mom if I could try to walk back to my room. My mom thought that since the nurse had said it was okay, I would be fine. I hadn't walked without my physical therapist yet so I was a little nervous. I lifted myself out of my wheelchair with the help of my mom and slowly started walking back to my room. We were almost back to my room when all of a sudden, I lost all feeling in my legs, and I collapsed to the floor. I had temporarily gone paralyzed. My fall was really bad and I hit the hard hospital floor with my legs twisted in really awkward positions. I was so scared and started crying thinking I had somehow become paralyzed again. My mom panicked and yelled for a nurse. Two nurses came running over and helped me back up into the wheelchair. I ended up breaking my ankle and cracking my kneecap. Seconds later, I got feeling back again so I felt the pain from the fall. I was so happy and relieved when I got feeling back in my legs. As if my recovery wasn't already hard enough, now for the rest of my hospital stay I had to relearn how to walk with a broken back, broken ankle, and a broken kneecap. Not fun at all. To this day, I still panic or freak out if my foot or leg goes numb because I think I'm going to be paralyzed again. I have never been diagnosed with it, but I am convinced I have PTSD from that accident. I have major panic attacks in cars, and I freak out whenever we get too close to the back of another car. I also go into a major panic if I feel like something is physically wrong with me etc.

When I was released from the hospital I was in a big back brace, which I had to wear for 6 months. I also wasn't allowed to drive which sucks when you're 16 and supposed to be getting your license. I had to use a wheelchair anytime there might be significant walking as my back was still very fragile and I had to keep limited in my movements. I was in constant physical pain, but I tried my hardest to power through it. I remember being at home and waking up in the middle of the night with awful back spasms that would last hours. I would wake up screaming and sweating from nightmares from the accident. It was a tough recovery, physically and emotionally. I was home schooled for awhile since I couldn't go back to school because I couldn't walk around for too long, and I wouldn't have been able to sit very long in a classroom at a desk. I loved being home schooled. I learned more in those few months of home schooling than I had learned in private or public school up until that point. I learn a lot faster in one-on-one environments. My homeschool teacher made learning fun.

After months of a grueling recovery, I was finally ready to go back to my private school at Los Angeles Baptist. I still had to wear my back brace though, and I was very self-conscious about it. I wore big hoodies to try and cover it up so the kids at my school wouldn't see it. I was so scared that the kids at school would make fun of me or think I was ugly because I had to wear a big ugly brace. I was back at school for only a few weeks when my biggest fear would come true. One day I was standing at my locker and Kevin, a popular football player, started making fun of my back brace in front of a bunch of people. I was so mad at him and completely humiliated that I took my full water bottle and threw it at his face as hard as I could. It was a stupid idea because I really hurt my back when I did that. I played softball and had a really good throwing arm so my water bottle ended up hitting him right in the middle of his face breaking his nose. I didn't mean to break his nose, I was just so angry and didn't think about it before I did it. I showed him right? Not really, guess what happened? If you guessed that I got expelled, you're right! Another school I got kicked out of and back to the mental hospital I went. Fortunately, I was only in the psych ward for a few days because with my injuries it wasn't a safe environment for me to be in. Besides, my threat to kill that stupid football jock was just a silly threat, I didn't really want to kill him, and I'm sure they couldn't have taken me too seriously coming from a girl with a broken back in a back brace!

This is what I learned:

- Do not take life for granted; you never know what can happen to you in the flash of a second. When faced with life and death, things are really put into perspective. Hug the people you love right now, tell them you love them, you never know what can happen and it can happen to anyone, even you or your family.

- Do not *ever* get in the car with a drunk driver. Always wear your full seatbelt and don't take the top strap off, doing that is what made me paralyzed. I almost lost my life to a stupid decision I made. Having one night of fun is not worth the risk of losing your life—or your legs. I was so lucky, but not everyone is.

- Every day when you get out of bed in the morning and your feet touch the ground, say thank you. If you are in a wheelchair and do not have the luxury of being able to walk, when you wake up in the morning, say thank you for being alive and being able to see. We take some of the biggest things in life for granted, and it is not until those things are taken away that we realize how lucky we were to have them in the first place. Feel lucky now! Be grateful that you can walk, see, and hear. Be grateful for everything you have. You never know what can happen.

Chapter 9

Panic Attacks & Graduation

"If you want to live a happy life, tie it to a goal,
not to people or things."

ALBERT EINSTEIN

By this time, my parents were absolutely done with trying to put me in another expensive private school. So it was back to another "special" school for me, but this one was different. Surprisingly, it was much better than the last one and I actually liked it. It was the continuation school for Montclair College Prep. If that name sounds familiar, it's because I was kicked out of that one as well. They had opened a continuation school for kids that were bad and needed extra attention.

I loved this new school because I was able to take an art class with Montclair and I loved my art class and anything to do with art. I looked forward to that class and always had a love for most things art related. It was a simple thing that made me happy and it had always been a creative and expressive way for me to deal with things, whether they were good or bad. Not long after the semester started I was finally able to take my back brace off. My recovery was still slow but going quite well considering the extent of the damage. Life felt pretty good, I felt like a normal girl again, which most of the last several years were anything but good or normal. I wasn't on drugs anymore and I wasn't on any prescribed medicine either. Things were really looking up for me and in a positive direction. Even Misty was completely out of the picture now because of the incident of her accusing my dad of molesting her daughter. She was finally out of my life for good and I would never have to face her physical and mental abuse ever again. Since I was now happy about my life, and I was happy about the new school I was at, I wanted to try and make an effort to do well and get more involved. It was my last year of high school and I was a senior so I really wanted to make it count and push myself during my last remaining time in high school. I had missed so much of a normal, fun, high school life that I wanted to do it all this last year. I joined the co-ed softball team and the co-ed football team. I was more involved in this school than any other school I had ever attended. I even became activities coordinator and class president.

My grades drastically improved, and I got to do fun school projects.

I liked the teachers I had, and we had smaller classroom sizes where I could get the one-on-one help that I needed to learn and excel. The only thing I began struggling with was my eating disorder a little bit but it wasn't nearly as bad as before. It's not something that I was proud of, but I pushed myself to do a lot of other things well and move forward.

Things were good with me, but not so much for my parents that year. There wasn't any crazy drama, but they just weren't happy together so they decided to split up again. It was for the best, besides I had already dealt with that in the past so it wasn't as big of a deal for me this time around. I was more disappointed than anything, but I wanted them to be happy.

By this time it was spring and almost graduation time. I was so excited thinking that I would be graduating from high school in just a couple months! I was also looking forward to our camping trip to Buena Vista. It was our spring trip we did almost every year. My friend Erin and I drove out to the lake, which is about 2 hours away from home, and we were meeting my dad and some other family out there. As usual, we had so much fun out there waterskiing at the lake and camping. While we were there I met this guy named Joe. He was the hottest guy I had ever seen and he was into a lot of the same things that I was into. He rode dirt bikes and wakeboarded, and he was totally my type. We hung out a lot when we were camping, but I was really excited because he was from the same area that I was, the valley! I really liked him and knew we would be able to see each other when we got home too. Everyone camped at the lake for a few days and we all ended up having a really fun trip but it was now time to head home.

I drove my friend and I back, and as we got about half way home, we started over this mountain called "The Grapevine". It's a long steep mountain north of Los Angeles that you need to drive up and over. Suddenly as I was driving, I felt like I was dying. In an instant, I went from being completely fine to drenched in sweat. My heart began pounding fast and hard inside my chest. I couldn't breathe and I couldn't calm myself down. I thought this was the end, and everything in my body and mind said prepare for death. It was the scariest feeling I had ever felt, and I couldn't control it. I didn't know what was happening to me. In a panic, and within seconds, I slammed on the brakes stopping the car in the middle of the freeway. I didn't stop because there was traffic or another car in front of us. Nobody was in front of us. As soon as the car came to a stop I jumped out of the car, stood there panicked and staring at everything, yet nothing at all. Erin had no idea what was happening and she began to freak out and kept yelling at me to get back into the car. "What is wrong with you?! What is happening?!" she said. I couldn't answer because I didn't know. I was frozen in a panicked state of mind. I thought I was dead, or dying. It's a hard thing to describe. I felt like I was having a heart attack! A highway patrol officer saw part of what was going on and he pulled his car over to assist, but that didn't help me or go well. He thought I was on serious drugs. I hadn't taken any drugs though, and hadn't had any alcohol. Fortunately, he did help us because our car was still in the middle of the freeway. We caused a huge scene but thankfully nobody was hurt. Eventually I was able to calm down. We could only assume it was some sort of panic attack or anxiety attack. I had never had anything like that happen to me before and I had dealt with some serious sh*t in the past. That was the start of my panic attacks, which I still get to this day. Luckily, I didn't get arrested, nor did I get in too much trouble with the officer which was a surprise considering my behavior and the danger to others that I could have caused by stopping the car like I did. Erin ended up having to drive us home because I didn't feel safe enough to drive. We made it home safe and alive but now with a new fresh set of issues to deal with.

Soon after our camping trip was my senior prom! I was so excited, this was my first prom ever that I would be going to. As expected, Joe and I were now boyfriend and girlfriend and he was now the love of my life. I was very interested in art and fashion, and I wanted to be a fashion designer and was going to try and apply to get into Fashion Institute of Design and Merchandising once I was out of high school. Since I was so into fashion, and since I wanted my prom dress to be a one of a kind I decided to make my own dress for my prom! I made a light pink high low dress and wore a backwards Dickies trucker hat with a white bow tie and white heels. Joe wanted our outfits to be matching, so he took his white tux and spray painted it hot pink and then stenciled skulls and stars on it so that it matched my dress. It was my first and last prom I would ever go to, so how could it be any better? Would you maybe say being Prom Queen? Yep! I was Prom Queen at my senior prom. What a night, it was so much fun, and after so many schools and expulsions I got to enjoy a real prom with a real boyfriend. My senior year flew by so fast, and of course shortly right after prom was graduation day. I had somehow stayed in school long enough to graduate. There were so many times when I didn't even think I would live to see 16, let alone graduate from high school. My parents were so happy and proud of me; they couldn't believe I was graduating, and neither could I. It felt so good to be on stage when I was given my diploma, it was one of the proudest moments of my life. I had felt like such a failure and a screw up in the past. This was a big accomplishment for me. After my graduation ceremony, I walked outside and there was a car with my name on it and a huge pink bow wrapped around it! My dad bought me my first car as a graduation present. It was a white Chevy blazer and I loved it. I had never been happier in my whole life!

This is what I learned:

- You can recover from anything. Even if you do awful things and are made to suffer through the consequences of your bad decisions, there is always a way to recover. Find your way back to happiness because it is waiting for you.

- Happiness is a choice. A lot of my hard times were made harder because my brain was stuck in a negative mood all the time. You have to choose to see things in a positive light. The impossible is possible—I know because I survived my childhood. I walked when they said I would never walk again, and graduated high school after being expelled more than 10 times from different schools.

- When someone is having a panic attack, help them. That is some seriously debilitating stuff. I would not wish it on anyone. Yoga, running, cutting down on caffeine, and eating properly can help you manage panic attacks. I also have a video on my YouTube channel on how I cope with panic attacks and anxiety disorders. If you or someone you know suffer from this awful disorder, please watch that video; I made it for *you*.

Chapter 10

Becoming a Stripper

*"Life is like photography, you need
negatives to develop."*

ANONYMOUS

graduated high school when I was 17 years old. I didn't turn 18 until the end of summer in September. On my eighteenth birthday the insurance company had automatically awarded me $85,000 as a settlement from my car accident. I planned to use the money to get my own apartment and pay for college. I was still with my boyfriend Joe, and madly in love with him. He was everything to me, and I loved him more than anyone else I had ever dated. I wanted him to move in with me once I got my new apartment. We talked about it a couple months earlier and he agreed that once I had graduated from high school, he would move in. He was a few years older than me, so it was better to wait until I was 18 years old.

As soon as I had that $85,000 and it was in my bank account, I went crazy with it. I wasn't used to having that much money. That's a lot of money all at once for an 18-year-old kid. None of my teachers, parents, nor any classes in school had ever taught me about savings, budgeting, or investing, and if they did I was most likely ditching class that day so I had no idea about managing my money. So I bought anything and everything that I wanted. I found the nicest apartment I could find and rented it. I bought my boyfriend a brand new street bike. We went out to fancy dinners almost every night. I went shopping almost every day. I also paid for a semester of college at FIDM and that school wasn't cheap. Four months later, I ran out of money. I spent $85,000 in less than 120 days! I really screwed up, I wasn't thinking or paying attention to what I was doing. I had nobody to blame but myself and I took full responsibility for blowing through that money. I didn't want to tell my parents that I had spent all of my money. They would have absolutely freaked out on me and would have killed me! I didn't have a job at the time, as I was living on the money awarded to me. My boyfriend was pretty much a deadbeat pothead stoner who didn't have a job either and was basically living off me but I was so in love with him, and he was so good looking that I just looked right past it. When I told him that we were out of money, instead of talking about how we could make money as a couple, or even him offering to get a job and help out, he immediately suggested that I do amateur night at the local strip club so I could pay the rent and all of our expenses. I told him he was crazy and there was NO WAY I was going to do that. I was definitely not planning or wanting to do that, but Joe had a way of convincing me to do it. I still loved him, and wanted to make him happy, and even though I didn't want to do it, we did need money for rent and bills.

That same night happened to be amateur night at the strip club. I had made up my mind I was going to do it after all. I got really drunk at home first because I was so nervous. I put on my platform sandals, the shortest skirt that I owned, a Victoria's Secret bra, and a tank top. Then we headed over to the local strip club. It was the first time I had ever been to a strip club. It's kind of funny, my first time walking into a strip club was going to be so that I can dance on stage. Not to hang out, not to watch a friend dance, and not for a laugh or a fun night with friends watching strippers. I was the stripper that night, and the people were going to be watching me. I was beyond nervous. Even as drunk as I was, I was still nervous about the whole thing. Once we got inside I realized that my shoes and outfit were way off, but whatever, it was amateur night and I how was I supposed to know, I had never been in a strip club before. I had butterflies in my stomach backstage as it was getting closer to my time to go on stage. I thought what the hell am I going to do out there? What if people boo me off stage? What if they don't think I'm pretty enough to be up on stage? Anytime you're in front of people on any kind of stage or platform, regardless of what it's for, they judge you. They look over your entire body and rate you. It's really scary. They finally called my stage name and my music came on and I walked out on stage! Immediately people started cheering and whistling for me. All the support and cheering really helped my confidence and I wasn't so nervous anymore. I still had no idea what to do on stage though! Yes, I had escorted before, but dancing on a stage in front of a huge group of horny men is different. After about 30 seconds, I got really into my song that was playing, and I started dancing way better. I got a rush of adrenaline and a feeling of being high. It felt good, and it was kind of fun. I started to like it, and the power that I felt with it. Everyone was looking at me and admiring me, and while on that stage I felt like I belonged there. I felt accepted. It wasn't as bad as I thought it was going to be. I had fun on stage and I made a lot of tips, almost $100 in tips to dance to one song. I was kind of sad when my song was over I wanted to keep dancing. I couldn't believe I got paid to have fun. I watched a few of the other amateur girls dance on stage and I was blown away, these girls weren't amateurs, they were like acrobat performers! I had no idea you could do so many tricks on a pole. After I watched a few of them dance I knew I had no chance of winning that night. But I still had fun and I made $100.00! Not long after, I was getting ready to leave just as they were about to announce the winners for the night. Then I heard them call my name. To my surprise, I had won first place! I couldn't believe it. I won $1000 for first place. When I went into the manager's office to get my money, he told me that I did a really good job and asked if I wanted a job there. I said, "I would love to work here. I had so much fun!" I needed a job anyways, so I accepted. He smiled at me and said I would make a lot of money working there. I walked away with $1,100 cash in my pocket that night. It was almost enough money to cover rent. I was so glad I was offered a job, I didn't have to stress about paying bills or having to call and ask my parents for money. I could also still afford go to school. Life was looking brighter again. I spent four months dancing at that strip club until one night something happened that would change my life forever.

To be continued......

No one's life is perfect.

We all know that no one's life is perfect; in fact, Instagram, YouTube, movies and magazines make us sometimes believe that the people around us are living these perfect lives that are so much better than ours, and I just want to say IT IS NOT TRUE! Let me repeat that again so it is VERY clear, NO ONE'S LIFE IS PERFECT. Everyone goes through stuff, whether it be an eating disorder, being abused, having a drug problem, having divorced parents, the list goes on. Every one of you reading this book right now has been through some sort of traumatic event, maybe not as crazy as mine or maybe it's crazier. What is important for me to let you know is that you are not alone. I know personally I have felt so alone in this world, thinking that I was the most awful person on this planet and that my life would be a living hell as long as I lived but I wanted to share my story with you so that maybe you could relate to me in some way through my story, or maybe I helped you realize that you are going down the wrong path and you want to start being a better person. It is very important to me that I share my stories with people to let them know that whatever happens, there is always a way to reach the light at the end of the tunnel. I do not just want to share my story; I want you to learn from my mistakes.

Schools can be a hostile environment.

Perhaps school was once a safe, nice place to learn, but times have changed. Bullying is on the rise, and children can be cruel. Know that you are perfect just the way you are, and that people that say mean things to you may be jealous of you, or maybe they talk bad about you behind your back because they hope that other people won't think you are cooler than them. There are so many reasons people bully people but I believe the main reason is because the people being mean are the ones that hurt the most on the inside. My dad would always talk down to my mom, but today I realize he only did that because he had low self-esteem. So try to grow thick skin and know that it is not you, it is them. And just remember that I love you and you can come watch my YouTube videos if you need a good friend.

The psychiatric industry can be deadly.

This is a touchy subject for me because I believe I was wrongly medicated as a child and it really f*cked me up, but I also now suffer from anxiety and panic attacks and I rely on medication to help me with that once in awhile so I do think there are good and bad sides to psych meds. I think you need to be very careful when choosing a doctor because I believe the pharmaceutical company and doctors are overmedicating our society to make money. That is just my personal opinion. Be careful when being medicated, and try to live without it if you think you can. Do not trust every doctor just because they are a doctor. Not all of them have your best interest in mind; what they have in mind is growing their bank accounts. But again, I do think medication is great when used properly. Unfortunately, I think it rarely is.

Life is a precious thing.

You have heard it before. Life is precious. Somehow you managed to be born, and now you exist along with trillions of other "living" things in the universe. It is a gift and a responsibility. Either you can use your life to inspire, help others, leave a legacy, invent something awesome, spread positive messages, entertain others or you can use it to drag everyone you know and love into a pit of despair. It is your choice, and it begins with your mindset—how you perceive the world. If you are unhappy with the world you are living in, you need to change yourself and your way of thinking until you find your true happiness. The best part about finding happiness is that it all lies within you! Once you realize that no one else but you has the power to change your life, that is when you will know you are on the right path. You have the power to make your life exactly how you want it to be, you are the creator of your life, so make it freaking AWESOMESAUCE!

You can recover from a traumatic childhood.

For a long time I believed that I had been through too much to survive to adulthood, but I did. Traumatic childhoods are a great way to learn a lot when you are young. It's never something kids ask for, but once it's happened, it is important to know that there is life after the rubble clears. You can be anyone you want to be; your childhood does not define you.

Instead of blaming everything on your parents, forgive them. Instead of dwelling on the mistakes that you made when you were young, move past them. Life is not always fair, but it is forgiving. You can renew your faith in yourself and in the world by starting over. You might have to learn how to get along in a "normal" way, but that is just another great adventure. Life is fun! Make the best of it.

Choose happiness.

If I told you that you are the only one that can make yourself happy would you believe me? It is true, sure others can make you happy, but it is only temporary, you are the one that determines your happiness. Choosing happiness is about knowing how to get there. That means removing the obstacles keeping you from being happy and then challenging yourself to fight for that positive mindset. Train yourself to see the good first, even though seeing the bad comes naturally. Train your brain to see the glass as half full, not half empty.

I remember when I was younger I told my dad I wanted to be a doctor, he told me that the only kids that become doctors are the kids that get perfect grades and study medical books from a really young age. I know my dad didn't know it but in that moment I felt like I could never be a doctor. I let my dad influence my life because I didn't know that I had the power to do whatever I wanted.

Things are going to happen to you in your life, and how you react to them will determine your experiences. A happy person does not face any fewer challenges than you do; they simply choose to find the good and amplify it for their own self-care and sanity. You are important. Care for yourself and others, and always focus on the good things. You can do anything you want to do in life. I wish my parents had told me that. But because I know that not all parents are perfect and sometimes make mistakes or forget to tell us important things I want you to know that no matter how old you are, no matter what your grades were, what you have done in your past, that you CAN do and be whatever you want regardless of what anyone has told you. Only you can make it happen, so follow your dreams and do what makes you happy. Don't wait around for it to come to you; you have to go after it! What are you waiting for?!

Thank you so much for reading my first book. In my second book I will talk about being a stripper, what it was like, and how I went from stripper to porn star overnight. I will talk about what it was like to be a porn star, all the craziness, and how I eventually after 8 long years got out of the adult entertainment industry. Also, go check out my YouTube Channel, it is FREE and it is where I post all kinds of fun videos, such as daily vlogs (me filming my everyday life and what I am up to now), product reviews, beauty, fashion, and so much more:

www.youtube.com/channonrose1

I love you guys and I am sending you all my love and positive energy! MUAH!

Love, Channon Rose
xoxo

CPSIA information can be obtained
at www.ICGtesting.com
Printed in the USA
LVOW04s0736250916
506059LV00005B/25/P

9 781505 462685